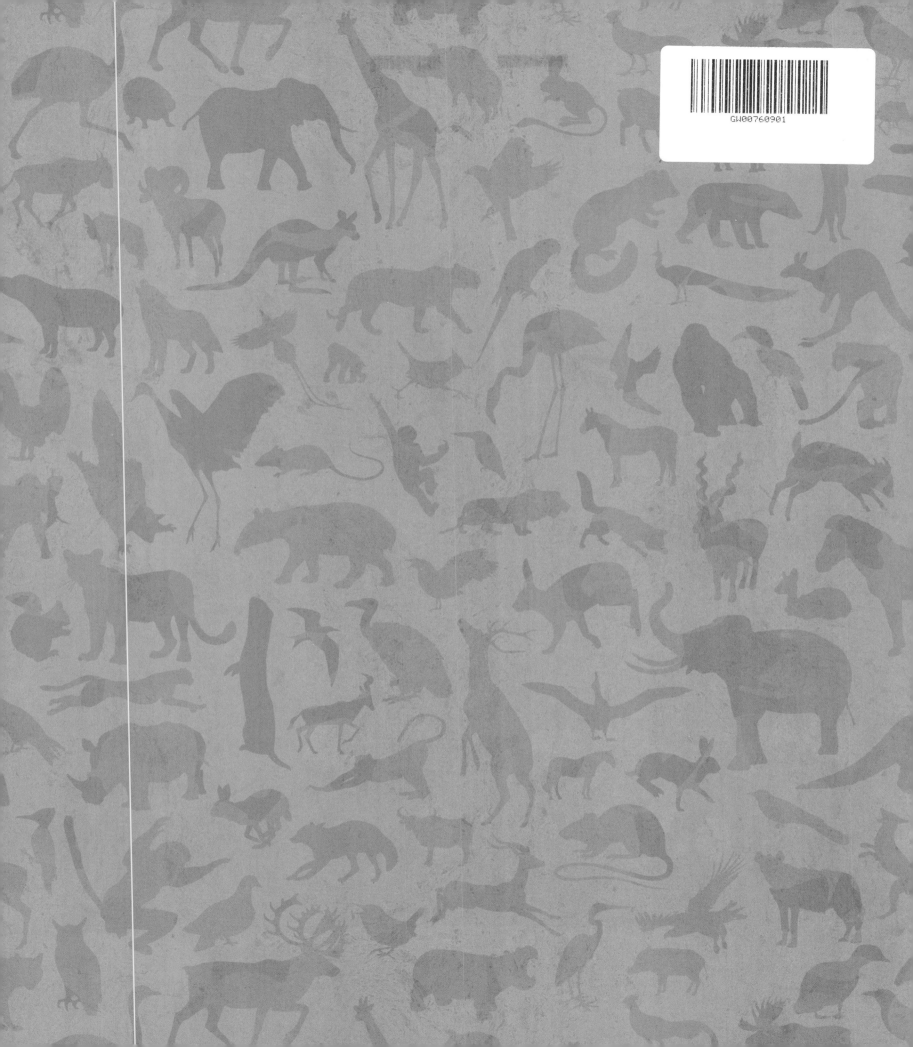

Incredible Journeys

AMAZING ANIMAL MIGRATIONS

KINGFISHER

First published 2011 by Kingfisher
an imprint of Macmillan Children's Books
a division of Macmillan Publishers Limited
20 New Wharf Road, London N1 9RR
Basingstoke and Oxford

Associated companies throughout the world
www.panmacmillan.com

A CIP catalogue record for this book is available
from the British Library.

For more information, please visit
www.kingfisherbooks.com

Conceived and produced by
Weldon Owen Pty Ltd
59–61 Victoria Street, McMahons Point
Sydney NSW 2060, Australia
weldonowenpublishing.com

Copyright © 2011 Weldon Owen Pty Ltd

WELDON OWEN PTY LTD
Managing Director Kay Scarlett
Publisher Corinne Roberts
Creative Director Sue Burk
**Senior Vice President,
International Sales** Stuart Laurence
Sales Manager, North America Ellen Towell
**Administration Manager,
International Sales** Kristine Ravn

Managing Editor Averil Moffat
Designer John Bull
Cartographer Will Pringle/Mapgraphx
Images Manager Trucie Henderson
Production Director Todd Rechner
Production and Prepress Controller Mike Crowton

ISBN 978-0-7534-3383-6

Printed by 1010 Printing International Limited

Manufactured in China

The paper used in the manufacture of this book is
sourced from wood grown in sustainable forests.
It complies with the Environmental Management
System Standard ISO 14001:2004

A WELDON OWEN PRODUCTION

animalplanet.co.uk
animalplanetbooks.com

Incredible Journeys

AMAZING ANIMAL MIGRATIONS

Dwight Holing

KINGFISHER

Contents

Land 14

Air 52

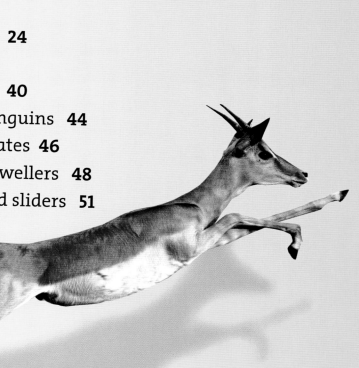

Water 88

Introduction

arth's seasons roll in an endless cycle, bringing winds, rain, heat and chilling cold. Some lands dry out under fiercely hot temperatures; others are covered by deep snow. For the creatures of the animal kingdom, life is a constant challenge. In the air, through the water and across land, wild, wonderful and intriguing animals are on the move. Their journeys in search of food, better weather and a safe place to bear their young are called migrations. And the story of how they manage to find their way is amazing.

Incredible Journeys is filled with such stories. Meet a bird that flies from pole to pole and back again – a yearly trip of nearly 80,000 kilometres. Follow a sea turtle hatchling, so small it would fit in your hand, as it cracks out of its egg, scrambles across a beach and catches a current that carries it across the ocean. See why a newborn caribou must hit the ground running if it is to keep up with its family and stay ahead of the wolves.

Come and explore a world where colourful birds and butterflies fill the sky, whales and sharks swim from sea to sea and herds of huge African elephants march tirelessly across the savannah.

The migration story

Year round and all over the world, animals of many kinds set out on remarkable seasonal journeys, or migrations. They travel – by air, water and land – to avoid cold, gather food or find safe places to give birth to their young. Some, like these North American caribou, take weeks to trek vast distances, while others move swiftly to another habitat or breeding area. Exactly how animals know where and when to go is still something of a mystery.

Escaping to warmer climates

Where winter brings severe cold and reduced food supplies, animals may leave for warmer places in autumn and return in spring. Migrations of this kind are common among highly mobile animals such as birds and marine mammals.

Whale of a trip After breeding through the winter in the warm Gulf of California waters, grey whales travel more than 8,000 kilometres to summer feeding grounds off Alaska.

Partial migration Among some bird species, such as the European robin, some members of a group may stay in one place all year, while others migrate for the winter.

Ducking out Mallard ducks live all over the Northern Hemisphere. Those that breed in the far north migrate south for the winter.

Ice flow Walrus follow the movements of the Arctic pack ice, migrating north as the ice melts in the summer and returning south as it reforms during the colder months.

Nomadic migrants In east Africa, huge herds of wildebeest (left) and smaller groups of impalas

A search for food

Food supplies are affected by rainfall,

A search for water

Not many animals, especially land animals, can survive for long without water to drink. So it's not surprising that shifting water supplies can prompt migrations, especially in arid zones and places with distinct dry and wet seasons.

Dry run In June, African elephants begin to migrate towards lakes and larger rivers that are less likely to dry out during the dry season, which usually lasts until November.

A journey to breeding grounds

To reproduce successfully, animals need plenty of food as well as a secure place to bear and nurse their young. Many animals migrate to the same location every year for this purpose.

Grasslands North American pronghorns migrate up to 240 kilometres to find snow-free grasses to eat during winter. They use long grasses to conceal newborns from predators.

Arctic nursery In the summer, caribou travel north by the thousands to calving grounds on the Arctic tundra. The plants that grow here help the mothers produce rich milk that makes baby calves grow.

Back again Twice a year, southern elephant seals migrate north from their hunting grounds off Antarctica to subantarctic islands, once to breed pups like this one and once to shed skin.

One-way trips

Usually migration is a round trip, but sometimes there is no way back. One-way migrations may involve a permanent move to new territory or a last long journey prior to death.

Home run After spending their adult life at sea, Pacific salmon return to the river where they were born to spawn and die.

Mass exodus If a lemming colony grows too crowded, a large group may migrate in search of new territory.

Solitary creatures Regional populations of blue whales migrate to and from the same summer and winter grounds. However, they normally travel alone or in pairs.

In groups or alone

Travelling in a group can allow animals to hunt together or provide a measure of safety. However, some animals travel alone because they prefer not to share scarce food or, especially if small, are less likely to be spotted by predators.

Long march Native to tropical South America, army ants migrate many times a year in search of food. Marching in columns as long as a football field, they devour any small creatures in their path.

Preparation and travel

Migrating to another habitat can be a risky business. The way may be long and filled with danger. Animals have to prepare themselves well and follow a route that will take them to their destination as swiftly, easily and safely as possible. Prior to departure, most creatures, like these grey whales exercising off Baja California, spend time building up their strength. Once on their way, they may travel nonstop or stop to rest, eat and drink along the way. While many migrants travel by day, others journey at night to avoid their predators.

Getting ready

Most animals gorge before departure to increase their energy reserves, and many exercise intensively to strengthen particular muscles. Some can even reduce the size of their internal organs to make them lighter for the trip.

Fuelling up Before they set off, migrants such as snow geese (far left) and hummingbirds (left) increase their body fat, the most efficient form of energy storage.

Well armed In response to overcrowding, locusts develop longer wings and prepare to migrate. They fly in huge swarms that may contain billions of insects.

Flying high White storks must travel by day because they rely on rising air currents, or thermals, to carry them from Europe to their winter grounds in Africa.

Routes and timing

The routes followed by migrating animals may be determined by the terrain, the availability of food and the climate. Timing a journey is critical, as even a short delay may mean missing a helpful tide or running into bad weather.

Pit stops Mountain meadows (below) and barrier islands (below right) provide migrants with places to feed and rest. Often, the same locations are visited on every trip.

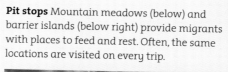

Predators

Well aware of the comings and goings of the animals they feed on, predators often gather along migration routes to feast on prey. Some rely on a greatly increased intake of food at such times to prepare for their own breeding cycles.

Feeding frenzy Between May and July each year, thousands of dolphins gather to feed on giant schools of sardines migrating north along the coast of South Africa.

On the wing Resident on Mediterranean islands, Eleonora's falcons delay nesting to hunt migrating songbirds, catching them in midair.

Mad dash On Christmas Island in the Indian Ocean, millions of red crabs migrate a short distance to the seashore to lay eggs. They swarm through forests and across roads to get there.

Short and long trips

The distances covered by different animals during migration vary hugely. However, even the shortest trips can involve surmounting major obstacles, while, on the other hand, some epic journeys may be plain sailing.

Sea way Humpback whales swim more than 13,000 kilometres from their high-latitude summer waters to tropical breeding zones.

Go with the flow

Animals use natural forces to help them travel faster and farther. Many winged creatures catch a lift on prevailing winds, while fish and sea mammals hitch a ride on tides and powerful ocean currents.

NORTH AMERICA

New York

Los Angeles

Wind power Monarch butterflies rely on autumn winds to carry them south to Mexico and spring winds to return them to the southern United States.

Riding the breeze Using their long wings to harness air currents, albatross can soar for vast distances using little energy.

Massive mover Weighing up to 6.4 tonnes and standing up to 4 metres tall, the African elephant is the largest land migrant.

Conveyor belt Turtles use Atlantic Ocean currents to carry them smoothly between far-flung feeding and nesting sites.

Record makers

	Species	Statistics
Longest round trip	Arctic tern	80,000km
Longest land trip	Caribou	6,000km a year
Longest insect trip	Monarch butterfly	4,800km in autumn
Largest migrant	Blue whale	Up to 33.5m long
Smallest migrant	Zooplankton	1–2mm
Fastest traveller	Common eider duck	Average speed 75km/h
Highest traveller	Bar-headed goose	Up to 10,000m

Finding the way

Animals can navigate over immense distances, often in complete darkness or the absence of landmarks, and, in some cases, even when they have never made the journey before. By tracking migrants using radar and other technologies, modern researchers have shown that animals adopt a variety of methods to find their way. These range from observing the sun, stars and wind patterns to sensing and following Earth's magnetic fields.

Screen scene Radar allows scientists to follow flocks of birds as they migrate. The radar screen above shows a snow geese flock near Winnipeg in Canada.

Sound map Whales send out sounds and use the echoes that bounce back to map out what lies ahead. This process is called echolocation.

Super senses

Animals have special senses that help them migrate successfully. Most have a built-in chronometer or timepiece that tells them when to depart, and some have specialized navigation tools.

Ocean obstacles Just like land, the seabed is covered with hills, ridges, peaks and valleys. Sea creatures must navigate through these landforms, often in pitch darkness.

Sumatra

Indian Ocean

Java

Java

Surabaya

Bali

Java Sea

Borneo

Trench

Shore guides Coastlines are long, recognisable landforms that can guide animals on their journey. Many birds migrate along coasts, and some whales stay close to them when travelling between their winter and summer ranges.

Signposts

At night, animals may use magnetism or the stars to navigate. By day, some, such as ants and starlings, are guided by the position of the sun. But most take a simpler approach and use familiar landmarks – mountains, rivers, lakes and so on – to tell them where to head, when to turn and where to stop.

River routes Rivers form pathways through landscapes. Migrating birds and bats follow them as do the creatures that live in their waters.

Landforms Birds often migrate along mountain chains. Valleys can provide clear corridors, and distinctive peaks indicate when to change direction.

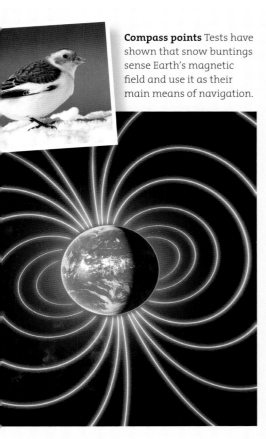

Compass points Tests have shown that snow buntings sense Earth's magnetic field and use it as their main means of navigation.

Animal magnetism A magnetic field surrounds our planet. This is the force that causes a compass to point to the North Pole. Scientists say some animals, including birds, bats, butterflies and turtles, have a built-in magentic compass. They use it to detect Earth's magnetism and guide them on their way.

The human factor

Human activities interfere with animal migration. Land clearance removes vital habitats. Roads, fences and pipelines block routes. But now people worldwide are learning more about animal migration and are helping in many ways.

In touch Tracking devices like the radio transmitter on this elk allow researchers to map migration routes and work out how best to protect them.

Loss of trees Clearing forests for timber or farms robs animals of a safe place to live or a suitable place to rest during long migration journeys.

Watch out Road signs are used to alert drivers to wildlife along many migration paths.

In the way Collisions with powerlines, towers and tall office buildings are thought to kill tens of millions of migratory birds every year.

Land

Journeys by Land

ANIMALS OF SAVANNAH, TUNDRA AND FOREST
The epic journeys of land animals make a spectacular sight. Wave after wave of wildebeest herds roll across a sea of grass in Africa. Caribou surge over Alaska's tundra in one continuous stream. Monkeys swing from tree to tree. Through deserts and forests, over mountains and across poles, migrating animals are always on the march.

Some land animals trek as far as 6,000 kilometres a year.

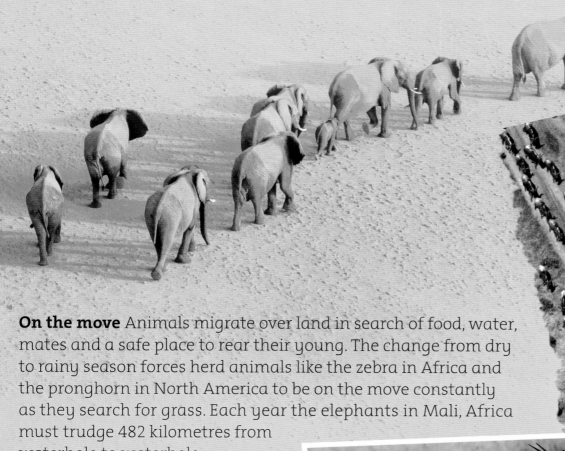

On the move Animals migrate over land in search of food, water, mates and a safe place to rear their young. The change from dry to rainy season forces herd animals like the zebra in Africa and the pronghorn in North America to be on the move constantly as they search for grass. Each year the elephants in Mali, Africa must trudge 482 kilometres from waterhole to waterhole.

Varied journeys Migrations are as varied as the species that make them. Some are as short as the week it takes a red crab to scuttle 8 kilometres across Christmas Island in the Indian Ocean to hatch its eggs. Wildebeest travel clockwise on a roughly circular journey 2,900 kilometres long on the Serengeti Plain in Kenya and Tanzania, Africa.

Great risks Unlike migrations through air and water, land animals cannot rely on help from currents. They must make the journey step by step. Though land animals' journeys are often shorter than those made by birds and fish, the risks can be higher. Rough terrain, extreme temperatures and dangerous predators abound. Cheetahs and lions lay in wait for passing herd animals, targeting the young and weak.

African elephants

Families on the move

Among the oldest and largest animal species still to walk the planet, African elephants are on a constant search for food and water. They eat on average 226 kilograms of plants and drink 190 litres of water a day. To find it all, elephants must make long journeys across the continent as the dry and rainy seasons change.

African elephant fact file

Type	Mammal
Family	Elephantidae
Scientific name	*Loxodonta africana*
Diet	Herbivore, prefers grasses and leaves
Average lifespan	70 years
Size	Up to 7.3m in length
Weight	6,000–9,000kg

Equipped for survival

The elephant has special features that help it survive as it migrates. Its massive size protects it from all but a couple of predators — lions and crocodiles. Both males and females have tusks, which are actually large, modified teeth used for fighting, feeding and digging. Elephants have a strong sense of hearing and can communicate with each other at distances of up to 10 kilometres away. A baby elephant can walk two hours after birth.

Skin
Thick and sensitive
While its rubbery skin is as much as 2.55 centimetres thick in some places, an elephant can feel a fly land on it.

Trunk
Strong and nimble
Both an upper lip and nose, the trunk has 40,000 muscles and can push down a tree or pluck a blade of grass.

Feet
Large and silent
With tough but spongy soles that act like shock absorbers, elephants walk over all types of ground.

Migration

Elephant herds are close-knit families led by one of the oldest and strongest females. Like a historian, she holds a mental map in her head about where the waterholes, food supplies and dangers lie in their home range, which can measure up to 2,000 square kilometres. Some herds travel as far as 480 kilometres a year.

Mating season — **Anytime**

Calving season — **22 months later**

Females and calves
Herds are made up of females and their young. Sometimes several herds join together and can number 100 individuals.

Across Africa
Elephants are found in a wide area of Africa. Three large migrating herds move through parts of Tanzania and Kenya, Mali, and Zambia and Botswana.

Elephant distribution
Large herds migrate seasonally

Cairo

Nile

A F R I C A

Equator

Congo

Atlantic Ocean

Indian Ocean

Cape Town

THE SEARCH FOR FOOD AND WATER
African elephants have large brains that serve like a GPS on the dashboard of a car. They store enormous amounts of information about routes from waterhole to waterhole and the feeding grounds between. Life is an endless loop of survival for elephants.

To the waterhole

Reduced range Once elephants roamed across most of Africa. Today, their range and numbers are much smaller. Human population growth, poaching, habitat destruction and changing climate are among the reasons why. The total population is estimated to be between 400,000 and 660,000. This includes two different species of African elephants. The most numerous and better-known kind dwells in grassland areas called savannahs in the eastern and southern regions. The other type lives in the forests of western and central Africa. Both species migrate.

Timing Migration begins at the start of the dry season. For savannah elephants that means June.

Family units made up of mature females and the young will break away from the larger herds and begin the trek. By travelling in smaller groups, they have a better chance of finding enough food and water along the route. A group is always led by the strongest and most experienced female. They walk in single file. Another dominant female brings up the rear. Her job is to supervise the young and guard against predators. Bull males also migrate, but alone and at their own pace. Calves born along the way are on their feet and joining the march within a few hours of birth. When the rains return, usually from October to December and March to June, the herds return to their native regions to feed on newly grown vegetation.

Elephants can find distant waterholes with pinpoint accuracy; it is key to their survival.

Zebras
The great trek

Zebras belong to the horse family and are instantly recognisable by their dramatic striped markings. There are three species of zebras, but the most common on the savannah is the plains zebra, also known as the common or Burchell's zebra. Zebras usually live in family groups of several females and their young, led by a stallion. Often, large herds of family groups will form when the time comes to migrate at the start of the dry season.

Zebra fact file	
Type	Mammal
Family	Equidae
Scientific name	*Equus quagga*
Diet	Herbivore, preferring long, tough grass
Average lifespan	25 years
Size	Up to 2.4m
Weight	220–322kg

Chase
The lion chases the zebra . . .

Zebras are among the lion's favourite prey. Lions cannot run fast for long so depend on getting as close as possible to the victim before making the final chase. The lion usually tries to separate out an animal from the rest of the herd.

Contact
Leaps to sink in its claws . . .

Once close enough, the lion rushes at its victim and seizes its rump with powerful paws equipped with sharp claws. The lion's aim is to get the zebra on the ground, where it can kill it with a bite to the neck or hold on to its throat until it suffocates.

Capture
And brings down its prey

The zebra is a powerful animal, too, with strong legs. It fights back with all its might and sometimes succeeds in seriously wounding the hunter as it kicks with its rear hooves. But the lion usually wins in the end.

Breeding

Calves are usually born during the rainy season and weigh about 32 kilograms at birth. The calf almost immediately struggles to its feet and can run within hours of birth. It starts to eat grass when it is a week old but continues to feed on its mother's milk until it is almost a year old.

Mating season
Aug–Sept

Calving season
Feb–Mar

Caribou
Tireless travellers

Caribou are the world champions when it comes to distance travelled by a land mammal. They live in the far north of North America, Europe and Russia. Each year they migrate between summer calving grounds and their winter homes. Some travel as far as 6,000 kilometres. Caribou can cover up to 55 kilometres a day and can run at 80 kilometres per hour. If a river or lake is in the way, they just swim across.

Caribou fact file	
Type	Mammal
Family	Cervidae
Scientific name	*Rangifer tarandus*
Diet	Lichen, sedges, willow leaves
Average lifespan	Up to 10 years
Size	Male: up to 2.25m; Female: up to 2m
Weight	92–210kg

Stalk
Patience and cunning ...
Wolves hunt in packs. They rely on surprise and numbers to catch the larger caribou.

Surround
Circle and separate ...
The pack singles out a mother and calf from the herd, then circles and separates the pair.

Attack
Feint and jab
Some keep the mother busy; unprotected calves are no match against the hungry pack.

Long trek The largest herds roam Alaska and northern Canada, migrating to the coast in the summer.

Migration

When spring comes to the Arctic and subarctic regions, groups of caribou join together to form huge herds numbering 50,000 to 500,000 animals. Like a river unleashed by a dam, they surge north to the calving grounds. In autumn, the herds break into smaller groups again for the return trip south to the sheltered forests.

Mating season	Calving season
Sept–Nov	May–June

Fur Two coats keep them warm in the winter; the outer layer has hollow hairs.

Antlers Males and females grow new antlers every year.

Body A compact body helps the animal stay warm, no matter how cold it gets.

Nose Large nostrils allow caribou to warm freezing air before it enters the lungs.

Toes Each foot has four toes that can be spread to act like snowshoes.

Hooves In the winter, footpads harden; in the summer, they soften to aid walking over tundra.

Built for snow and ice

From their noses to their spreadable toes, caribou are uniquely adapted to their harsh environment. Ears and tails are small to guard against freezing. Legs are short and powerful to run across snow and tundra. Hooves help them walk on ice without slipping and dig through snow for their favourite food, 'reindeer moss'.

Right of way

Even in the frozen north, caribou must deal with man-made obstacles, such as oil and gas pipelines, that can block their traditional migratory routes. To prevent disruption, pipeline systems provide passageways for caribou. The Trans-Alaska Pipeline System has more than 500 elevated sections and 20 buried locations, so animals can freely cross under or over.

NORTHERN GRAZING GROUNDS The annual trek of caribou from Canada to Alaska rivals the great migrations across Africa's Serengeti Plain. Three herds of 500,000 animals apiece, and countless smaller herds, make the trip. Seemingly endless lines of caribou arrive at the tundra to enjoy the summer. Thin after a long winter, they graze on a carpet of thick grass.

Summer in the Arctic

Arrivals The pregnant cows arrive at the grazing grounds first and almost all give birth in the first ten days of June. This is a defence strategy for the species. With so many babies born at once, predators like wolves and brown bears can barely make a dent in the population. But even so, calves are not just easy pickings. Within hours of birth, a baby caribou can run faster than a human. Summer is not all fun and sun. When the air warms, the wet tundra gives rise to thick clouds of bloodsucking mosquitoes and black flies. Caribou rush to coastal areas where cool sea breezes blow away the pests.

Meadows Lush meadows of cotton grass await the hungry herds, but late snow can still cover patches of the far north when calving begins.

Polar bears
Sea-ice specialists

Polar bears roam hundreds of kilometres each year in search of prey, moving onto frozen seas then back to land when sea ice melts. Theirs is a truly mobile home. Sea ice drifts with the currents and shifts between freezing and melting. While the Arctic's environment is harsh, it is far from lifeless. Areas of open water support plenty of life, including seals, narwhals, beluga whales and walrus. All are food for the polar bear, the world's largest meat eater that lives on land.

Polar bear fact file	
Type	Mammal
Family	Ursidae
Scientific name	*Ursus maritimus*
Diet	Ringed and bearded seals
Average lifespan	25 years
Size	Males: 2.4–3m; females: approx. half that
Weight	Males 350–680kg; females: approx. half that

Shared food Arctic foxes follow polar bears in the winter, hoping for leftovers.

Icy north
Polar bears migrate closer to the pole when the ocean freezes but retreat to the mainland in the summer.

Adapted for the Arctic

Polar bears reflect the unusual world they live in. Their white fur is the perfect camouflage for sneaking up on seals, their favourite food. It also helps keep them warm in freezing temperatures. The top coat is made up of hollow guard hairs that repel water. Beneath a dense coat of underfur is a layer of blubber 10 centimetres thick.

Claw Curved claws aid in digging in the ice and gripping seals.

Foot Large padded feet help with walking on ice and swimming.

Born on ice

Polar bears mate in April and May. During the next four months, the mother eats a lot, doubling her weight. Next, she digs a den and hibernates. She bears her cubs between November and February.

The den The mother digs a den in snowdrifts or in permafrost.

Long stay The family stays inside until spring; the mother does not eat the whole time.

The litter There are usually two cubs in the litter. At birth they weigh less than 1 kilogram.

Entrance The den is entered by a very narrow tunnel.

ICE FLOES AND OPEN WATER Polar bears spend most of their time wandering across large chunks of ice floating in the Arctic Ocean. But that ice is now melting under their feet faster than ever. Global warming is to blame. Over the past 30 years, the Arctic ice cap has shrunk by a size equal to nearly one-third of the continental United States or one-fourth of all of Europe. This has a huge impact on Arctic wildlife, especially polar bears. Scientists predict that two-thirds of polar bears could disappear by 2050 if the melting trend continues.

Loss of the ice cap

Warmer temperatures caused by greenhouse gases are melting sea ice faster, shrinking the polar bear's frozen world.

Disappearing ice The melting ice cap is already causing problems for polar bears. Food sources are growing scarcer, and the bears are becoming thinner. The population, which now numbers between 20,000 and 25,000, is declining. In Hudson Bay, Canada, warmer temperatures and shrinking ice has cut the seal-hunting season by nearly three weeks. The average polar bear living there now weighs 15 per cent less than before. The Hudson Bay population has dropped by 20 per cent. The shrinking ice cap is also expected to lead to problems for the bear's main prey, seals. Seals eat fish, and changing temperatures alter fish populations, too.

Swimming Polar bears typically swim from ice floe to ice floe and between land and pack ice. They are especially strong swimmers. The hollow hairs in the outer layer of fur help keep them afloat. But as the ice melts, they have to swim greater distances through open water, sometimes for days on end and for more than 100 kilometres before reaching ice or land. More and more polar bears are drowning as a result.

Desperate swim As the ice cap melts, bears have to swim farther to find food. Many cubs drown.

Catching seals

The Arctic is home to millions of ringed and bearded seals. Polar bears depend on the two species for survival. They spend much of their waking hours hunting and eating the blubbery creatures in order to build up their own fat reserves. The bears hunt mostly in places where the ice meets the open water.

Waiting Polar bears rely on their strong senses of smell and hearing to locate seals.

Ready to strike The bear smells the seal's breath, jabs its paw into the hole and hauls the seal out.

Successful catch Dragging it onto the ice, the bear kills the seal, biting its head and crushing its skull.

Emperor penguins
A cold march

Emperor penguins are birds that don't fly and spend most of their time swimming. But it is their march across ice every year to breed and bear their young that makes them even more amazing. Penguins must shuffle and toboggan on their bellies to complete their long journeys, for many up to 200 kilometres one way. Once the chick is born, parents must make the trip over and over again to bring it food.

Penguin fact file	
Type	Bird
Family	Spheniscidae
Scientific name	*Aptenodytes forsteri*
Diet	Fish, krill and squid
Average lifespan	20 years
Size	Up to 122cm tall
Weight	22–45kg

Freezing winter
Emperor penguins and their chicks remain on the Antarctic continent throughout the winter.

Antarctic Circle

ANTARCTICA
+ South Pole

Antarctic Circle

A cold wait
The chicks are hungry

Penguins are born in one of the coldest places on Earth. The mother lays the egg, but the father incubates it. He balances it on top of his feet for nine weeks, careful never to let it touch the ice. Older chicks are left alone while their parents hunt.

Parents return
The successful hunters

With their torpedo-shaped bodies, penguins are designed more for swimming than walking. Getting onto the pack ice to return to their chicks requires shooting out of the water and making a bellyflop landing.

Feeding time
A welcome meal

The parents catch a variety of species on their fishing trips, often swallowing the prey whole. Back at the nesting grounds the parent regurgitates the food, giving the chick a warm, liquid meal.

Forest primates

Treetop dwellers

Not all migrations are long journeys or on set routes. In rainforests, such as those on Borneo in southeast Asia, primates keep moving from tree to tree. For them, it is a never-ending race to reach ripening fruit before it is found by others. The forest vegetation is dense, and the fruit is often far above the ground. Finding food is never easy. For an animal that cannot fly, reaching it requires special abilities.

Gibbon

With long hands and feet, and wrists with ball-and-socket joints, gibbons can swing from tree to tree faster than other primates. They reach speeds up to 55 kilometres per hour.

Orangutan

The orangutan is the largest primate living in trees. It has the longest arms, but it is not a graceful swinger. Instead, it uses its weight to sway one branch closer to the next.

Red leafs

Red leaf monkeys don't swing but walk along tree limbs and branches on all fours. They travel in noisy groups of up to 12 individuals led by a dominant male.

Forest fruit
Rambutan are a favourite food for many species of primates. Family groups migrate through the forest, searching for the fruit in season.

Hands and feet

Like humans, primates have skilled hands and feet for grasping that sets them apart from other animals. Their fingers and toes move easily and have sensitive pads at the tips and nails instead of claws.

Primate hand An opposable thumb can push against the other fingers to aid in gripping.

Primate foot The big toe is set apart from the other four, allowing for a strong grasp on branches.

Other species

The tropical rainforests of the world support dozens of species of fruit-eating primates. With few exceptions, they are foragers, travelling high and low through the jungle in search of food.

Gibbon White-handed gibbons have hooked hands for speedy movement by swinging.

Monkey The proboscis monkey often walks on the ground as well as travelling through trees.

Macaque Long-tailed macaques leap between trees, using their long tails for balance.

Mountain dwellers
Vertical migration

Some migratory routes are up and down rather than north to south or east to west. This is the case for animals that live in steep mountains, like Dall sheep and mountain goats in North America and takin in central Asia. But, as with other migrants, one of their main reasons for migrating is the search for food. In the winter, animals typically move to lower elevations; in the summer they seek the high ground.

Grazers Takin live in the Himalayas and graze in bamboo forests and alpine meadows.

Dall sheep These agile sheep can leap small streams as well as climb steep, rocky walls.

Special hooves The takin's two toes spread apart like fingers, making climbing easier. Special pads provide traction.

On the prowl

Steep slopes provide some protection, but mountain dwellers must always be on the lookout for predators like the snow leopard that stalks wild goats and sheep in central Asia's mountain ranges. In North America, the danger comes from wolves, coyotes, bears and golden eagles.

A dash of salt

Mountain sheep and goats eat a wide variety of plants during the summer, but in the winter their diet is limited to mostly dry, frozen grass and lichen and moss. In the spring, animals look for natural salt licks, such as the one on this rocky cliff, to supplement their diet.

Butting heads

Male Dall sheep sport thick, curling horns that grow continually and are never shed. Rams hold head-butting contests to establish leadership in a herd. The duels can go on for hours. Females have horns, too, but theirs are shorter, more slender and less curved.

Life on a slippery slope

Mountainside migrants must keep a tight grip to survive.

WILD GOATS AND SHEEP

The four-footed inhabitants of the high country are uniquely adapted to its dizzying heights. They need the ability to climb, leap and not slip. They must also be able to stay warm and out of reach of predators. Dall sheep's cloven hooves make them sure-footed while scaling rocky slopes, steep cliffs and outcrops. Their eyesight is like a human using binoculars.

High altitude Mountain goats live in North America as far south as the Rocky Mountains. They rarely come down below the treeline. The tips of their feet have a special claw that is sharp and helps them to avoid slipping. Double-layer wool coats keep them warm, even when winter temperatures drop to −46°C and winds blow as hard as 160 kilometres per hour. Kids are born in the spring and start running and climbing within hours of birth.

Scuttlers and sliders

Christmas Island crab and red-sided garter snake

Not all incredible land journeys are made by warm-blooded animals. Certain types of insects, reptiles and crustaceans migrate, too. Their trips are sometimes among the shortest, but that doesn't make them any less difficult or dangerous. Big or small, creatures migrate in search of food, mates and a safe place to bear their young.

Island fever

On Christmas Island in the Indian Ocean, millions of red crabs migrate from the forest to the sea in November. The trip is only 4 kilometres, but it takes a week to complete. At the shore, males dig burrows, find mates and breed. Females stay for two weeks, then lay their eggs in the sea and scuttle back to the woods.

Snakes alive

In central Canada during the winter, thousands of red-sided garter snakes hibernate together in underground dens. They awake when the summer comes, and the males slither away as far as 20 kilometres to hunt frogs. Females go, too, to give birth to as many as 50 live young each. They all return when the weather turns cold again.

Air

BIRDS, INSECTS AND FLYING MAMMALS

Look up in the sky. Chances are you will not have to wait long. A wedge of geese, a charm of finches or a murder of crows will soon fly by. Birds are always on the move, especially in the autumn and spring. That is when millions take to the air on annual migrations. Birds are not the only ones, though. Bats, bugs and butterflies migrate, too.

Journeys by Air

Strong headwinds and sudden storms can challenge aerial migrants on epic journeys.

On the wing Birds will fly incredible distances to reach their destination. The Arctic tern travels from pole to pole to enjoy not one, but two summers each year, a flight of about 40,000 kilometres. Even the tiniest birds will undertake extreme trips. The ruby-throated hummingbird is not much bigger than your thumb, but it flies 20 hours nonstop over 724 kilometres of open ocean to reach its favourite breeding grounds.

Following flyways Birds travel the equivalent of a highway in the sky when they migrate. These great aerial routes are called flyways. The Pacific flyway in North America and the central Asia flyway are just a couple. Most flyways are over land, providing travellers with plenty of stops along the way to rest and refuel. A few are strictly ocean routes, like those used by albatross and shearwaters.

Danger waits Migration poses perils for all birds, no matter if they are as big as a crane or as small as a warbler. Predators like hawks and falcons can ambush the unwary. Storms can strike at any time. Hunters wait in fields for ducks and geese to land. Birds must avoid obstacles, from power transmission lines to mountaintops.

Ravenous horde
Locusts swarm fields by the millions in search of food. Bats migrate in huge numbers, too.

Flyways

CROWDED SKIES The migration of billions of birds across thousands of kilometres every year is one of the natural world's greatest marvels. While some birds may flit from area to area in search of more food, only the regular seasonal journeys of certain species are called migrations. There are more than 10,000 bird species in the world, and nearly half migrate. They follow invisible routes called flyways and stay on course by using various navigation systems, including following physical markers and charting the stars.

Rufous hummingbird
This tiny hummingbird must find nectar along the way from Alaska to Mexico

Locust

Monarch butterfly

ARCTIC

NORTH AMERICA

ATLANTIC OCEAN

Least bittern

American kestrel

The Atlantic flyway
Around 200 species of birds breed in North America in the summer and migrate to South America in the winter. The Atlantic flyway is a key migratory route, used by the least bittern, Cape May warbler, American kestrel and rusty blackbird, among others. No mountains block the route, and it offers good sources of food and water for a journey that can range from 640 to 16,000 kilometres.

PACIFIC OCEAN

SOUTH AMERICA

Arctic tern
This long-distance flier travels between the poles, 20,000 kilometres each way.

Rusty blackbird

Laughing gull

Cape May warbler

American redstart

European white stork
Big wings help the stork catch a lift on thermals of hot air along the Black Sea/Mediterranean flyway.

Eurasian teal
This pretty duck breeds in Eurasia and migrates south for the winter.

Eastern curlew

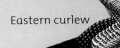

Eastern curlew and Latham's snipe
These two intrepid travellers wing their way from northeast Asia to eastern Australia.

Latham's snipe

Short-tailed shearwater
This hearty bird breeds in southeast Australia and makes an annual migration around the Pacific Ocean.

OCEAN

EUROPE

ASIA

PACIFIC OCEAN

AFRICA

Common cuckoo

Common cuckoo and barn swallow
Both birds migrate along age-old and heavily used routes between Eurasia and Africa.

OCEANIA

Bat

Barn swallow

Black Sea/Mediterranean flyway This is one of three main flyways that connect Europe to Africa. Crossing 101 countries, it is used by more than 6 billion birds representing 300 different species.

INDIAN OCEAN

SOUTHERN OCEAN

ANTARCTICA

Wandering albatross
Albatross dominate the skies of the southern oceans. With their extra-long wings, they spend most of their time aloft, rarely touching down.

Seabirds

Short-tailed shearwater and wandering albatross

Some seabirds hardly ever stop flying. They make quick work of long distances, able to cross entire oceans in weeks. Aerodynamic bodies and the ability to land and take off on water helps them not only survive but master their watery world. The short-tailed shearwater is a member of a group of 60 medium to large seabirds. There are 21 different types of albatross. The wandering albatross is the largest.

Short-tailed shearwater fact file	
Type	Seabird
Family	Procellariidae
Scientific name	*Puffinus tenuirostris*
Diet	Krill, squid, fish
Average lifespan	15–19 years
Size	60cm
Weight	510–600g

Shearwater

Named for their ability to slice through the air, shearwaters are graceful fliers. Around 23 million breed in southeast Australia, most on the island of Tasmania. The female lays a single egg in a deep burrow. Both mates take turns incubating it. Parents leave on a long migratory flight when the chicks are still covered in down. Two to three weeks later, the young birds follow, finding the way on their own.

Streamlined Long, narrow wings are good for high-speed gliding.

Migration

These migrants circle the Pacific, flying north around the western edge to spend the summer in the Arctic region, then returning southward to Australia, flying straight across the middle of the ocean. They travel about 15,000 kilometres each way every year. Shearwaters can complete a one-way trip in just six weeks.

Breeding season	Hatching season
Sept—April	January

Albatross

These ocean wanderers have the largest wingspan of any living bird, measuring up to 3.5 metres across. Long wings come in handy as they patrol the cold southern waters in search of food. Early sailors considered these birds good omens. Today, populations are declining and the albatross is vulnerable to extinction.

Wandering albatross fact file

Type	Seabird
Family	Diomedeidae
Scientific name	*Diomedea exulans*
Diet	Fish, cephalopods
Average lifespan	Up to 50 years
Size	Up to 135cm
Weight	Up to 12kg

Single egg The wandering albatross breeds every other year.

Migration

The wandering albatross circumnavigates the southern oceans. The birds migrate between subantarctic and subtropical waters. Breeding and rearing young takes place mainly on islands off Australia, South Africa and South America. After fledging, the young take to a life soaring over the ocean, returning to breed.

Breeding season
Nov—Jan

Hatching season
March

Glands Salt glands help birds get rid of saline from ingested seawater.

Tendon sheets Tendons at the shoulder lock the wing so it can be kept outstretched when soaring.

Designed to soar

Everything about the wandering albatross's body is designed to aid in its life soaring close to the water's surface. It is so adapted for this lifestyle, it can fly for hours at a time without flapping its wings.

Heart rate The bird's heart rate stays the same at all times.

Bones Light bones can bear the stress of take-off and landing.

Big feet The feet are completely webbed, and there is no hind toe.

SUPERB DESIGN The fastest sailboats use sails modelled after albatross wings for good reason. They are long, stiff and streamlined, perfect for catching and holding the wind. Albatross spend 80 per cent of their life at sea. They only visit land to breed and bear their young. The birds can reach speeds of up to 135 kilometres per hour and can glide hundreds of kilometres without flapping their wings. They do this by using a clever trick that grabs energy from the wind and allows them to soar great distances.

Sailing seabirds
Albatross are master gliders. They skim over the ocean catching uplifts of air.

Winged sailors

AFRICA

SOUTH AMERICA

ANTARCTICA
+ South Pole

AUSTRALIA

Raising young Graceful and powerful in the air, albatross move awkwardly on land. Their nesting colonies are built on barren and windswept islands. The big birds perform elaborate dances to attract mates, pointing their bills skywards and raising their long wings. It takes a lot of effort to raise a chick. Parents will fly thousands of kilometres to find enough food for just one feeding. Taking off from land requires a lot of energy, too. Birds must run while flapping their wings. Once airborne, though, they let the wind do all the work and sail away.

Albatross ride the wind over the sea for months at a time.

Shorebirds

Winged waders

Shorebirds are one of the biggest families of birds on the planet. There are more than 400 different species. Most migrate. Many are known for their extraordinary feats of flying, winging their way from the northern reaches of the Arctic to below the equator and back again. Some complete annual journeys of up to 24,135 kilometres. While many follow the coastline, a few, like the bar-tailed godwit, fly straight across oceans.

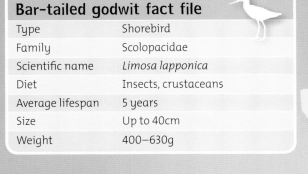

Bar-tailed godwit fact file	
Type	Shorebird
Family	Scolopacidae
Scientific name	*Limosa lapponica*
Diet	Insects, crustaceans
Average lifespan	5 years
Size	Up to 40cm
Weight	400–630g

Bar-tailed godwit

This slender, long-beaked shorebird holds the endurance record for nonstop flight. It flies 11,680 kilometres from Alaska to New Zealand. The crossing takes a week of nonstop flying. Riding a tailwind at high altitude speeds the journey and shortens the flight time by half.

Arctic breeders
Godwit chicks are ready to fly across the Pacific Ocean at two months old.

Flock safety Flying in large flocks protects individual birds from attack by predators.

Beaks speak

True shorebirds are generally distinguished by long legs, no webbing between their toes and unusual beaks. Some beaks are long; others are short. Some curl up; some curl down. It depends on the bird's feeding strategy. Probers, such as godwits, use long beaks to probe for buried clams and crustaceans.

Northern lapwing

A member of the plover family, this common shorebird migrates throughout Europe and Asia, wintering as far away as Africa and China. It travels mainly during the day in huge flocks and feeds at night on insects and worms plucked from farmland and mudflats. The bird's wings make a lapping sound when in flight.

Nest defence Eggs are laid in small scrapes in the ground or in low grass. Parents noisily attack all intruders. The chicks remain with their parents for up to 40 days, until their first flight.

Arctic terns

Long-distance flier

Arctic terns are the kings of the bird world when it comes to commuting. Every year they fly from the top of the globe to the bottom and back again. Depending on where they summer and winter, the round trip can be as much as 80,000 kkilometres. Given that some terns live into their thirties, that is the equivalent of making three round trips to the Moon over a lifetime, or 60 times around Earth.

Arctic tern fact file

Type	Seabird
Family	Sternidae
Scientific name	*Sterna paradisaea*
Diet	Fish, invertebrates
Average lifespan	20 years
Size	33–39cm
Weight	86–127g

Ready to fly

Terns breed in Arctic regions. Courtship starts with ritual displays. Females chase males high into the sky, and afterwards, males offer females a fish. Parents mate for life. Nests are usually small scrapes on bare ground, sometimes lined with shells or grass. Eggs hatch in about three weeks, and three to four weeks later, the young are ready to fly. Within three months, they are winging their way south.

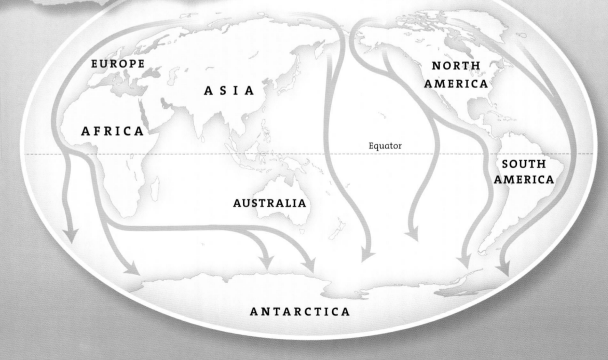

Migration

In August, terns leave their summer grounds from Iceland to Alaska to escape the cold, dark polar winter. A marathon flight takes them to the bottom of the world, where it is summer. Terns journey north again in April and May, taking advantage of prevailing winds to make the journey in about 40 days.

Breeding season   Hatching season

May–June   June–July

The sea Terns never venture far from the sea. They breed in solitary pairs or colonies of up to several hundred pairs.

Fast and strong

Forked tails and wings that are longer than they are wide help terns hold in place as well as fly fast and far. The birds keep an eye out for small fish and shrimp swimming close to the surface. When they spot food, they hover, wheel, then dive, catching their prey with their beaks. Sometimes terns chase down insects in the air or steal food from other birds by dive-bombing to force them to drop their catch.

Foraging In Antarctica, terns forage near icebergs and pack ice and in channels between ice floes.

Swallows

Barn swallows and relatives

Swallows migrate by the millions. This family of birds is among the most populous, with 83 species. Swallows breed on every continent except Antarctica. They are known for their aerial acrobatics when feeding on insects. In Europe and North America, swallows leave their breeding grounds when winter approaches and insect populations drop. They head for warmer climates, where flying bugs are plentiful.

Barn swallow fact file	
Type	Passerine
Family	Hirundinidae
Scientific name	*Hirundo rustica*
Diet	Insects
Average lifespan	4–6 years
Size	17–19cm
Weight	16–22g

Violet-green swallow

Barn swallow

Cliff swallow

Silhouettes

Swallows have streamlined bodies and long, pointed wings that allow them to make quick turns and steep banks when chasing insects. The birds can reach speeds up to 65 kilometres per hour. Depending on the species, tails are forked, indented, or squared, but all have 12 feathers. Longer tails serve to attract mates and help with manoeuvrability.

EUROPE

ASIA

NORTH AMERICA

Equator

AFRICA

AUSTRALIA

SOUTH AMERICA

ANTARCTICA

Food on the fly
Swallows typically catch insects in the air but can pluck them off the water.

Barn swallow

Barn swallows are the most common swallow. They number up to 190 million and live throughout the Northern Hemisphere. Barn swallows prefer fields, pastures, and meadows near water. This gives them plenty of opportunities to find flying insects. When hunting, barn swallows usually zoom about 8 metres off the ground.

Tree swallow

These blue and white beauties breed in North America and winter in Central America, Mexico and the Caribbean. They are very social birds, sometimes gathering in groups of several thousand near roost sites. Flocks of one million have been recorded. Roosting in large numbers protects against predators like kestrels.

Energetic Swallows rarely sit still. They spend most of their waking time hunting insects.

Barn swallow

Tree swallow

Cliff swallow

Nesting

Swallows build a wide variety of nests. Tree swallows move into tree holes that may have once housed a woodpecker. Barn swallows build mud nests near the ceiling in old buildings. The most famous are those made by cliff swallows. They build the bird equivalent of apartment buildings out of mud. Their nests stick to the sides of cliffs and beneath overhangs, including bridges.

Violet-green swallow

Shiny purple and green feathers make this swallow stand out. It breeds only in the western part of North America and travels in huge flocks to Central and South America when the weather turns cold. Its favourite meals are mosquitoes, butterflies and moths. Violet-green swallows live in open woodlands and nest in tree cavities.

Commonplace Violet-green swallows are common throughout western America.

Cliff swallow

These tiny migrants travel some of the longest distances among all swallows. They wing between North America and Argentina. Cliff swallows became famous for returning like clockwork every year to San Juan Capistrano, California. There, they built mud nests beneath the eaves of an old Spanish mission.

BIG FLOCKS Common in both town and countryside, swallows gather on wires and tree branches when they're not busy chasing insects. These songbirds are often the first to migrate in the autumn. When temperatures dip and insect populations drop, swallows begin heading to warmer climates. Migrants typically cover about 322 kilometres a day. The journey is filled with danger. Swallows in Europe have to cross the Sahara to reach their wintering grounds. North American swallows face hundreds of kilometres of ocean before they can land.

Hardy globetrotters

Swallows are widespread The breeding range for some of the 83 different species expanded when humans began building structures and clearing forests. This led to more colony sites around the world. Swallow nests made with pellets of mud are common on the underside of bridges and beneath the eaves of barns. New reports, however, show climate change can affect swallow populations. The birds need the right amount of rain for wet mud to build nests. Too much cold means fewer insects, which means less food. Hot and dry weather causes heat stress and dehydration.

S̲wallows gather in huge flocks that swirl like clouds just before roosting for the night.

Mud homes Cliff swallows collect mud from puddles to build nests out of the reach of predators.

Flamingos

Night fliers

Flamingos do not reside only in zoos. Six species live in the wilds of Africa, Asia, Europe, North America and South America. The largest is the greater flamingo. The smallest is the lesser flamingo. The long-necked, long-legged birds spend most of the day feeding. When an area no longer provides enough food, flamingos will take wing at night and migrate to another location under cover of darkness.

Greater flamingo fact file	
Type	Flamingo
Family	Phoenicopteridae
Scientific name	*Phoenicopterus roseus*
Diet	Invertebrates
Average lifespan	20–30 years
Size	140–150cm
Weight	Up to 10kg

Taking off

Flamingos are strong fliers — once they get airborne, that is. Take-off is not easy for such tall creatures. They start by running straight into the wind with their wings outstretched to gather speed. Once off the ground, they flap rapidly, rarely stopping to glide. In flight, pink flamingos are quite a sight with their long necks outstretched and their equally long legs trailing behind. They fly in large flocks.

Migration

Some colonies are resident year round, but most are nomadic and migrate short distances to breeding grounds or when water and food become scarce. European flamingos travel to warmer locations in the winter. Asian populations relocate from inland lakes to coastal wetlands. In Africa, flamingos follow the rains.

Breeding season	Hatching season
March—July	27 days later

Specialized filter

Flamingos use their large beaks to filter small food items from the water. The beak is shaped like the keel of a boat, and tiny hairs cover plates, like baleen on a whale. The flamingo stirs up the silty bottom with its feet, then lowers its head into the water, upside down. Moving from side to side, it collects small shrimp and molluscs.

Why pink?

The bird's colouring reflects its diet. The food it eats contains carotene, a pigment that makes carrots orange. These pigments break down in the liver and are deposited into the skin and feathers. Colours range from pale pink to crimson. Caribbean flamingos have the reddest feathers. Chilean flamingos are among the palest.

Tall bird Long legs allow the flamingo to wade into deeper water than most other birds, an advantage when looking for food.

European white storks

To Africa for the winter

The myth that storks deliver babies comes from this bird's habit of building nests atop houses in Europe. After laying their eggs and hatching their young, storks head for Africa to spend the winter. Huge flocks make the journey together. Depending on their route and final destination, it can take as little as three weeks. The big birds spread out from Uganda to South Africa before returning north in the spring.

European white stork fact file

Type	Stork
Family	Ciconiidae
Scientific name	*Ciconia ciconia*
Diet	Fish, amphibians, reptiles
Average lifespan	25 years
Size	100–115cm
Weight	Up to 4.4kg

EUROPE

ASIA

AFRICA

Equator

Migration

White storks take one of two routes from Europe to Africa. One leads across the Strait of Gibraltar. The other crosses the Bosphorus to Turkey. Most birds choose the eastern route, even though it is longer, to avoid crossing the Sahara. Other bird migrants join them. These flocks can stretch for 200 kilometres.

Breeding season
Feb—April

Hatching season
33 days later

Travel hazard

Bad weather is not the only danger migrating birds face. They must also avoid colliding with man-made structures, such as powerlines and wind turbines. Scientists estimate millions of birds die every year by flying into such obstacles.

Stopover

Storks must stop often to refuel. Unlike some migrants, these travellers don't build up fat reserves before migrating. This helps them glide more efficiently. The trouble is, more and more places where storks used to stop to grab a meal are being turned into farms and cities. Wildlife groups and governments are working to solve the problem. The result is a project that aims to create a chain of special places along the migration routes so storks and other birds can eat and rest.

Good fishing

The long-legged waders are skilled at catching fish, but there are few animals a white stork will not dine on. Favourites include frogs, lizards, amphibians, moles, shrews and even young birds. Beetles, grasshoppers, locusts, and crickets are on the menu, too. White storks hunt mostly during the day. If the catch is small enough, they will swallow it whole. Bigger prey is cut up with their scissor-like bills.

Nesting sites

White storks are famous for their nesting habits. Males arrive first to choose an existing nest or build a new one. Some have been used every year for a century. The nests are made from sticks. They can be huge. A typical nest measures up to 1.5 metres in diameter and can weigh as much as 250 kilograms.

Welcome Storks are considered a good omen. People erect poles and platforms to help them nest.

Social creatures
Storks form large colonies. In Africa, they can number as many as 1,000 birds.

Common sight
Nests are seen on church steeples and chimneys in many towns in Europe.

Cranes

Migrants in danger

Cranes rank among the world's tallest flying birds. They are also among the most endangered. Nearly all of the 15 species are threatened with extinction due to loss of habitat in both breeding and wintering grounds. Cranes live on every continent except Antarctica and South America. The most species are found in Asia, where they are considered sacred. The red-crowned crane is the national symbol of Japan.

Red-crowned crane fact file

Type	Crane
Family	Gruidae
Scientific name	*Grus japonensis*
Diet	Amphibians, aquatic invertebrates, insects and plants
Average lifespan	20 years
Size	140–150cm
Weight	Up to 10kg

Dance moves
All cranes engage in dancing, usually as part of courtship. Red-crowned cranes dance more than most.

Red-crowned crane

The population of the red-crowned crane, the heaviest of all cranes, is estimated to be only 2,750, making it the second rarest in the world. There are two main breeding populations. One lives on the Asia mainland in northeast China and southeast Russia; the other lives on an island in northern Japan.

Migration

Only the mainland population of red-crowned cranes migrates. Following the breeding season, they fly to their wintering ground along rivers and in marshes in Korea and central China. The population in Japan stays within a radius of 160 kilometres season after season.

Breeding season   Hatching season

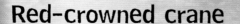

Spring & summer   29–34 days later

Home building Cranes build their nests on wet ground or in shallow water.

Life partners Cranes usually mate for life. Both parents incubate the eggs.

Habitat All cranes depend on healthy wetlands for food, nesting, overwintering, and stopovers when migrating.

Plane help To form a new migratory flock, an ultralight is used to guide the birds.

Balance To fly well, birds must have most of their weight in their centre of gravity.

Propulsion The wing's downbeat stroke moves the wingtip forwards and downwards.

Whooping crane

The whooping crane is the most endangered crane species. It also has one of the longest migrations. Once found from central Canada to Mexico, and from Utah to the Atlantic coast, only one self-sustaining flock exists today. It breeds in the Northwest Territories, Canada, and migrates to Texas.

Riding the air currents

CURRENTS Air currents sweep over the globe as ocean currents do through the water. Birds take advantage of them when migrating. A tailwind can push them farther and faster, in some cases cutting in half the time it takes to reach their journey's end. When it comes to a headwind, however, birds must ride currents up and down, just as sailboats do when they zigzag back and forth into the wind. Soaring birds use air currents called thermals and updrafts to help hold them aloft and carry them along.

Soaring birds save energy when they migrate by catching free rides on air currents.

Hot air Birds know that hot air rises. Updrafts of warm air are called thermals. It does not have to be summer to cause one. Even on cold days, the sun will heat the dark surface of a street a few degrees more than a field of white snow next to it. The rising air can lift light objects like feathers. Birds stretch their wings and ride these invisible warm clouds up in spiralling circles. When they reach the top, they fold their wings and glide down to the base of the next thermal, repeating the process over again.

Warm air riders

Hawks, cranes, storks and other soaring birds time their migrations and chart their routes to take advantage of thermals. Getting a lift from one warm current to the next makes their long-distance travels easier.

Songbirds

Tiny travellers

Four thousand of the world's 10,000 bird species are songbirds. They include sparrows, finches, warblers and swallows. Many are the world's smallest migrants, like the tiny willow warblers that fly between Europe and Africa. Songbirds have a special vocal organ that allows them to sing. Each species has a different song. Most sing while perched. The songs signal identity and territory.

Yellow warbler fact file

Type	Songbird
Family	Parulidae
Scientific name	*Dendroica petechia*
Diet	Insects
Average lifespan	10 years
Size	13cm
Weight	11g

Blackpolls The summer is spent in Canada and Alaska, then, in the winter, these birds fly across the Gulf of Mexico to South America.

Energy use

Songbirds can fit in the palm of your hand, but they are mighty fliers. Some log over 500 kilometres per day and can make the journey from Brazil to North America in two weeks. Having pointed wings and avoiding high winds helps. Migrating takes a lot of energy, more than normal flying. A songbird travelling 4,800 kilometres from Panama to Canada must beat its wings more than three million times.

Yellow warblers
These warblers breed in the United States then fly as far south as Brazil for winter.

Dangerous wind

Migration is the most dangerous event of the year, but climate change could pose new problems. An increase in high winds would force songbirds to use more energy. They would need to stop more often to eat. This could delay their arrival and the start of the breeding season. Worse, they could run out of fuel over the Sahara Desert or the Atlantic Ocean and never arrive at all.

Exhaustion Birds are sometimes blown off course and lack the energy to continue.

Togetherness Songbirds flock together for survival. Many birds means many eyes looking out for predators.

Kirtland's warblers These birds were nearly extinct, but the population is slowly recovering after conservation efforts.

Willow warblers Common throughout Europe, they migrate by the millions to sub-Saharan Africa.

Whitethroats These birds have a scolding song and nest across Europe and west Asia. In the autumn, they are off to the tropics.

Global Tiny birds that wing from Europe to Africa and back prove ecosystems are connected no matter how distant they are.

Amazon The rainforest in Brazil provides plenty of food, water and sunshine for birds escaping the northern winter.

Waterfowl

Web-footed fliers

Ducks, geese and swans are waterfowl. Worldwide, there are about 150 species. During migration, some fly just a few metres above the water, while others fly as high as 6,100 metres above sea level. Every year, millions follow a chain of lakes and fields on their long journey. In summer, they breed and nest up to the Arctic Circle. In autumn, they take wing to stay ahead of the winter's freeze.

Canada goose fact file

Type	Goose
Family	Anatidae
Scientific name	*Branta canadensis*
Diet	Grasses, grains
Average lifespan	20 years
Size	Up to 110cm
Weight	Up to 6.5kg

Canada goose

This species is known for its distinctive black head and white cheek patch, loud honk and V-shaped flying formation. There are 11 races of Canada geese. Most head to the north of Canada and Alaska in the summer to breed and fatten up. More and more, however, stay at their wintering grounds all year. They are now used to humans and feed in city parks.

Danger Waterfowl look for a refuge from foxes, but a goose will charge if a predator threatens.

Widespread The Canada goose is a large and widely distributed species of waterfowl.

Migration

Canada geese gather in flocks of up to several thousand to migrate. They fly in a V to help save energy and cover longer distances. The leader breaks the force of the air, which spares the followers from having to flap so hard. The birds take turns in the front. Canada geese can travel 1,000 kilometres a day.

Breeding season   Hatching season

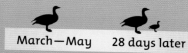

| March—May | 28 days later |

Snow goose

These noisy birds do not honk but bay like hounds. There are two forms: one has white plumage; the other bluish-gray. The birds breed north of the treeline in Canada, Alaska, northeastern Russia and Greenland. In the winter, snow geese fly south to parts of the United States and Mexico. Their favourite stopovers are farms in the Midwest, where they eat wheat, corn and other grain crops.

Fly high There are more than six million snow geese. In the spring, large flocks fly 4,800 kilometres north.

*D*ucks form huge rafts of thousands of birds on the water, then take off all at once.

Butterflies

Delicate dancers

The monarch butterfly rules the air when it comes to long-distance travel by an insect. Starting in August, millions across North America make a mass migration to California and Mexico to avoid the first frost. These tiny fliers flutter as far as 4,800 kilometres. A northbound migration from overwintering locations occurs in the spring. Australian monarchs migrate too, but for much shorter distances.

Monarch butterfly fact file	
Type	Butterfly
Family	Nymphalidae
Scientific name	*Danaus plexippus*
Diet	Plant nectar
Average lifespan	2 months
Size	Up to 10.2-cm wingspan
Weight	Up to 0.75g

Monarch butterfly

A monarch has four stages of life. Eggs hatch as larvae, then become caterpillars, then pupae. Finally, they emerge as butterflies. This process is called metamorphosis.

Caterpillar

Pupa

8–14 days

15 seconds

5 minutes

15 minutes

2 hours

Transformation The change from caterpillar to butterfly takes two weeks.

Migration

Only monarchs born in late summer or early autumn migrate south. They navigate with a chemical compass in their antennae that uses the Sun and Earth's magnetic fields for positioning. A butterfly does not live long enough to complete the entire return trip. Instead, it goes as far as it can, lays eggs, then dies. The next generation continues the trip where it left off. It can take four generations before the butterflies reach their final destination.

Homecoming
Millions of migrating monarchs often return to the same tree from which their ancestors once originated.

Dragonflies

In autumn, thick clouds of green darner dragonflies swarm down the east coast of North America. They are among the 50 species of dragonflies known to migrate. Green darners are only 7.5 centimetres long and have four wings. They get a boost from favourable winds and follow shorelines, cliffs and river valleys on their journey. It is a one-way trip. Migrating adults die after laying their eggs.

Midair meals
Dragonflies are winged predators. They zip around catching moths, mosquitoes and other flying insects.

Life cycle
Green darners deposit eggs in water plants. Eggs hatch into nymphs, which crawl out of the water to turn into dragonflies.

Compound eye Dragonfly eyes have 30,000 facets.

Bats

Winged mammals

Bats are plentiful and not very scary. Only three of the 1,100 species living worldwide are vampire bats that feed on the blood of birds and animals. Most bats eat insects. The others feed on fruit. About 30 species migrate to and from summer roosts and winter hibernation caves. Most do not go very far. The Mexican free-tailed bat takes the longest journey, which is about 1,800 kilometres each way.

Mexican free-tailed bat fact file

Type	Bat
Family	Molossidae
Scientific name	*Tadarida brasiliensis*
Diet	Insects
Average lifespan	18 years
Size	9cm
Weight	12.3g

Migration

The Mexican free-tailed bat is widespread. One of the biggest concentrations is in Texas. The bats only live here during spring and summer months. Starting in October, they fly south to Mexico. Sometimes they fly at 3,000 metres or so to catch prevailing winds to ease their journey.

Mating season	Bearing season
March—May	May—July

True fliers Bats have webbed forelimbs that have developed as wings. They are the only mammals that can fly.

Dwellings Bats roost in caves, crevices and even buildings. A cave in Texas houses 20 million Mexican free-tailed bats.

Locusts

Plagues and swarms

Desert locusts live in hot, dry places from northern Africa to India. They are a type of grasshopper, but they behave very differently. Every now and then the population explodes. The resulting swarm will sweep across huge areas and destroy valuable croplands in their path. The largest swarms can cover an area of up to 1,000 square kilometres and contain 40 billion locusts.

Desert locust fact file

Type	Insect
Family	Acrididae
Scientific name	*Schistocerca gregaria*
Diet	Plants, grasses, seeds
Average lifespan	3–6 months
Size	Up to 7.5cm
Weight	2g

Crowd Locusts change into a 'gregarious phase' when rain produces an excess of plants. They gather and breed in large numbers.

Desert swarm

A locust swarm is a type of migration. It, too, is in response to weather, breeding and the search for food. Swarms typically move in a clockwise direction on either side of the Sahara and Arabian deserts. They travel at the speed of the wind and can cover 100 to 200 kkilometres in a day. Swarms eventually die out when the food disappears, the weather changes or when birds and disease take their toll.

Water

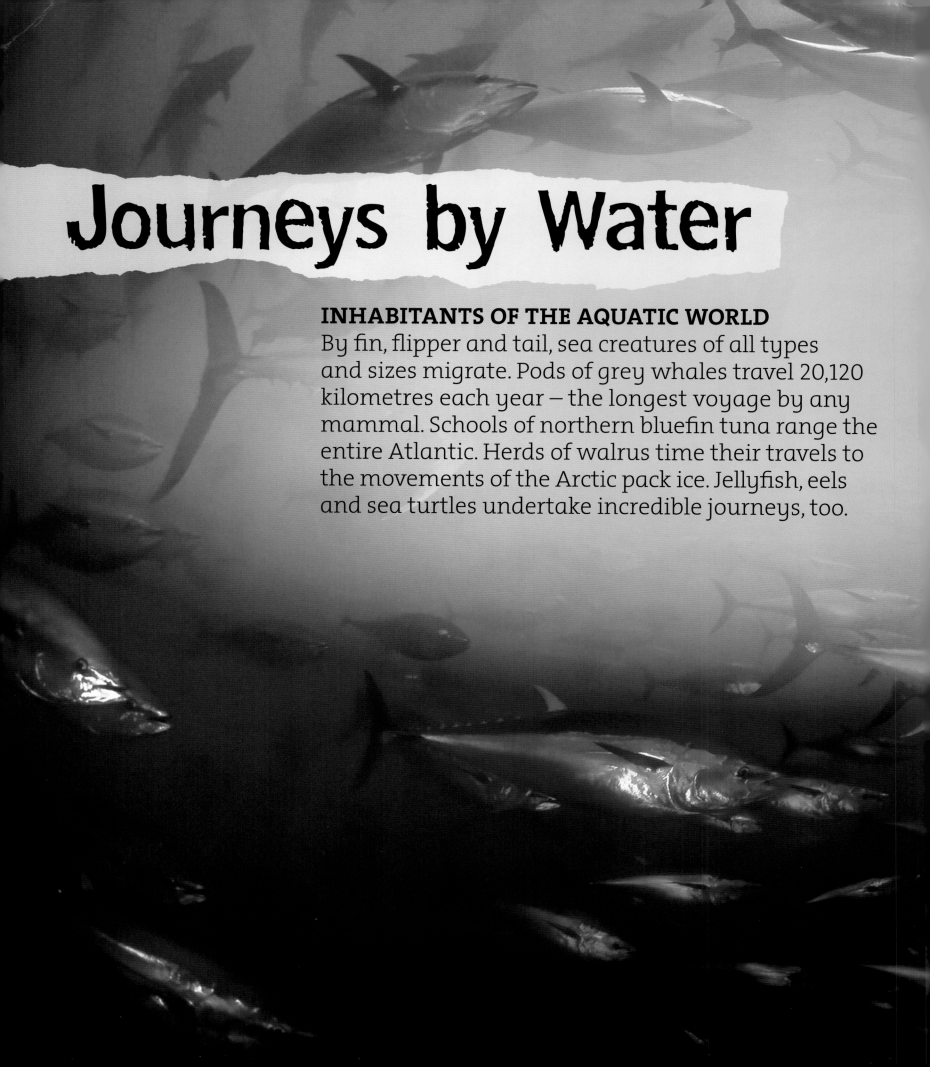

Journeys by Water

INHABITANTS OF THE AQUATIC WORLD

By fin, flipper and tail, sea creatures of all types and sizes migrate. Pods of grey whales travel 20,120 kilometres each year – the longest voyage by any mammal. Schools of northern bluefin tuna range the entire Atlantic. Herds of walrus time their travels to the movements of the Arctic pack ice. Jellyfish, eels and sea turtles undertake incredible journeys, too.

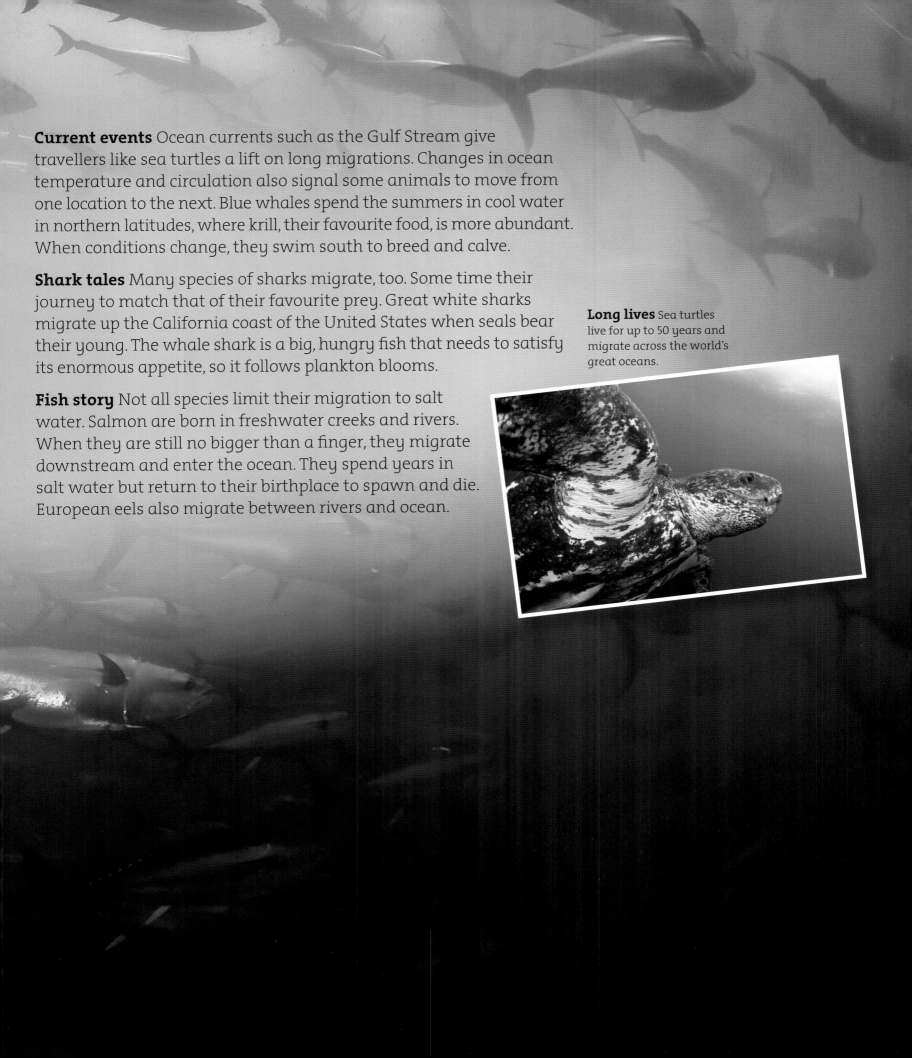

Current events Ocean currents such as the Gulf Stream give travellers like sea turtles a lift on long migrations. Changes in ocean temperature and circulation also signal some animals to move from one location to the next. Blue whales spend the summers in cool water in northern latitudes, where krill, their favourite food, is more abundant. When conditions change, they swim south to breed and calve.

Shark tales Many species of sharks migrate, too. Some time their journey to match that of their favourite prey. Great white sharks migrate up the California coast of the United States when seals bear their young. The whale shark is a big, hungry fish that needs to satisfy its enormous appetite, so it follows plankton blooms.

Fish story Not all species limit their migration to salt water. Salmon are born in freshwater creeks and rivers. When they are still no bigger than a finger, they migrate downstream and enter the ocean. They spend years in salt water but return to their birthplace to spawn and die. European eels also migrate between rivers and ocean.

Long lives Sea turtles live for up to 50 years and migrate across the world's great oceans.

Blue whales

Giants of the deep

Everything about a blue whale is big. They are the largest animals ever known to have lived on Earth – even bigger than the biggest dinosaur. Fully grown whales average 25 metres in length and weigh upwards of 109 tonnes. Their tongues weigh as much as an elephant. Their hearts are as big as a car. Blue whales are big swimmers, too. They travel from ocean to ocean around the world.

Blue whale fact file

Type	Baleen whale
Family	Balaenopteridae
Scientific name	*Balaenoptera musculus*
Diet	Krill
Average lifespan	80 years
Size	25m
Weight	109 tonnes

Big babies Blue whales are born big. A calf weighs 2,700 kilograms at birth and drinks up to 570 litres of milk a day.

Arctic Ocean

Atlantic

Ocean

Equator

Indian
Ocean

Pacific

Ocean

Southern

Ocean

Winter breeding areas

Migration routes

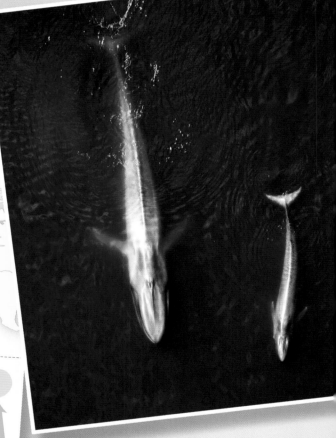

Migration

Blue whales usually live alone, but they will travel long distances to find mates, moving from polar waters to the tropics. Scientists believe they find each other by vocalizing. They have the loudest call of any whale and can hear each other from up to 1,600 kilometres away.

Mating season   Calving season

Oct–Nov   May–June

Feeding

Blue whales have baleen – fringed plates of material like fingernails that are attached to their upper jaws. Their favourite food is a shrimp-like creature called krill. They eat by gulping huge mouthfuls of water then squeezing it out through their baleen using their giant tongue. All the krill left behind get swallowed. A blue whale eats up to 40 million krill a day – about 3,600 kilograms.

Dainty diet Despite being bigger than a railway carriage, blue whales eat the tiniest food.

Krill There are 85 species of krill.

Tail fluke

Blue whales are big divers. They need to be if they are going to find enough krill, which are always moving at various depths. During the day, blue whales feed about 100 metres below the surface. They stay underwater for 10 to 20 minutes at a time. A powerful kick from their flukes helps them get down. Flukes are at the end of the tail and measure 7.6 metres across. Blue whales can swim as fast as 50 kilometres per hour.

Grey whales

Winter in California

Grey whales are easily spotted from the shore. They hug the coastline while migrating between their summer feeding grounds in the north Pacific and their winter breeding and calving areas in Mexico. They feed in shallow water by diving to the bottom, rolling on their side and sucking in sediment and water. When they close their mouth, baleen plates trap crustaceans and tube worms on the inside.

Grey whale fact file	
Type	Baleen whale
Family	Eschrichtiidae
Scientific name	*Eschrichtius robustus*
Diet	Crustaceans
Average lifespan	50 years
Size	Up to 16 metres
Weight	36 tonnes

Feeding Calves drink up to 300 litres of their mother's milk per day.

Summer Grey whales go north for the summer.

Migration

Grey whales start a journey of 8,000 to 11,000 kilometres south to Mexico when ice begins to form in the Bering and Chukchi seas. They begin arriving in the lagoons of Baja California in late December. For the next three months, they calve, nurse their young and mate. In March, they steam north again.

Mating season   Calving season

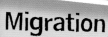

Dec–March   Dec–March

Fins Grey whales have no dorsal fin. Instead, they have a dorsal hump followed by up to 12 raised bumps that run to their fluke, or tail.

Flukes A mature whale's tail fluke can measure up to 3.7 metres across. It is notched at the centre.

Humpback whales

Song and dance

Famous for their singing and acrobatics, humpbacks live in oceans and seas around the world and migrate between polar and tropical waters. Humpbacks get their name because of the way they arch their backs out of the water when getting ready to dive. They can reach depths of up to 210 metres and hold their breath for 30 minutes. Humpbacks feed by gulping mouthfuls of plankton and small fish.

Humpback whale fact file

Type	Baleen whale
Family	Balaenopteridae
Scientific name	*Megaptera novaeangliae*
Diet	Krill, small fish
Average lifespan	45 to 50 years
Size	Up to 16m
Weight	36,000kg

Singing whales Male humpbacks sing. A typical song lasts from 10 to 20 minutes, though they can sing all day and night.

Migration

Humpbacks live in polar waters in the summer. When the winter approaches, they migrate to tropical waters to breed and give birth. Once they begin the long trip, there is no stopping. They can cover 1,600 kilometres a month. There is no eating during the winter, either. Instead, they live off their fat reserves.

Mating season

Dec–April

Calving season

Dec–April

Water acrobats

Humpbacks arch and twirl when they breach, slapping the water as they splash down. Standing on their tails and poking their heads out of the water is called spyhopping. These moves may be for play, to shake off sea lice or to communicate.

Long fins Unusually long fins help the humpback manoeuvre, and they provide temperature control.

Tails Each whale has unique markings on its tail, which can be used to identify individuals for study.

Great white sharks

Sea wolf

Great white sharks are the largest predatory fish on Earth. They hunt fish, seals, dolphins and even whales. Great whites live mainly in coastal waters, with the most found offshore of the United States, South Africa and Australia. They get their common name from their white underbelly; their scientific name means 'ragged tooth'. Great whites speed through the water like torpedoes.

Great white shark fact file

Type	Shark
Family	Lamnidae
Scientific name	*Carcharodon carcharias*
Diet	Seals, fish
Average lifespan	30 years
Size	Up to 6m
Weight	Up to 1,900kg

Food-rich waters
Australia's southern coasts support many great whites.

Migration

The migratory behaviour of the great white shark is mostly a mystery. Recent studies show they do not migrate just up and down the coast. Some travel long distances, such as between Baja California and Hawaii. Another study tracked a shark from South Africa to Australia and back.

Mating season	Pupping season
Various	11 months later

Jaws!

While great white sharks are portrayed as man-eaters, that is mostly the stuff of movies. Shark attacks are usually a case of mistaken identity — the shark confuses a diver or surfer for a seal. Still, great whites have sharp senses for detecting prey. They can smell one drop of blood in 95 litres of water and can sense even tiny amounts up to 5 kilometres away. Great whites can detect electromagnetic fields generated by animals.

Jaws The jaws hold 300 teeth arranged in rows. New teeth replace lost or broken ones.

Function Upper teeth cut and saw. Lower teeth are used for impaling.

Saw-edged The teeth are razor sharp and can be 7.5 centimetres long.

Whale shark

A whale shark can grow to be more than twice the size of its cousin, the great white. While both are fish, they feed very differently. The whale shark has a huge mouth, up to 1.8 metres wide. It is located at the front of its head, not on the underside like great whites. While it has teeth, the whale shark does not use them for eating. Instead, it feeds by holding its mouth open as it swims, vacuuming up plankton and filtering it through its gills.

GENTLE GIANTS Whale sharks are as big as a school bus, with a mouth so wide you could swim in it. Though they have 300 rows of tiny teeth, they do not bite. The big filter feeders are so gentle they sometimes even let divers hitch a ride. Their skin can be up to 10 centimetres thick, and each shark has a unique chequerboard pattern of pale yellow spots and stripes that does not change with age. Whale sharks can live as long as 100 to 150 years.

Coral Reefs off Australia's west coast attract migrating whale sharks in March and April, when coral spawn during a full moon.

Whale sharks

Long journeys Following plankton blooms, whale sharks travel thousands of kilometres each year. Though they can dive as deep as 700 metres, they prefer to stay close to the surface. Whale sharks live in warm water on both sides of the Equator. Favourite places are along coastal reefs and in the lagoons of coral atolls off Western Australia, Central America, and islands in the Indian Ocean. Groups join up off the coast of Papua New Guinea in September, then migrate to Australia in November and December. Little is known about their breeding habits, but females give birth to live young; they do not lay eggs.

Sensors The whale shark has poor eyesight, but sensors that run along its body detect pressure changes, giving it backup vision.

Northern bluefin tuna

Fatty but fast

Northern bluefin tuna are the speedsters of the Atlantic. They can reach bursts of 72 kilometres per hour. Even their cruising speed is fast — 48 kilometres per hour. Being quick gives them the advantage over their prey. The largest of eight tuna species, northern bluefins are built for endurance as well. Journeys from northern feeding grounds to southern spawning areas can be 10,500 kilometres each way.

Northern bluefin tuna fact file

Type	Fish
Family	Scombridae
Scientific name	*Thunnus thynnus*
Diet	Fish, squid
Average lifespan	15 to 20 years
Size	2m
Weight	250kg

Warm-blooded

Unlike most fish, bluefins are warm-blooded. The ability to regulate their temperature comes in handy. They can swim in the cold waters where they feed and the warm waters where they spawn. Their colours provide camouflage from above and below.

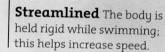
Streamlined The body is held rigid while swimming; this helps increase speed.

Good blood flow Core muscles are kept warm, helping bluefins swim in cold water.

Swift growth The tuna's high metabolic rate helps it grow.

Migration

Northern bluefin tuna range across the Atlantic when feeding. They swim as far north as Greenland and as far south as the waters between Brazil and southern Africa. Their spawning areas are limited to two locations. One is in the Mediterranean; the other is in the Gulf of Mexico. Female bluefins produce up to 30 million eggs.

Spawning season

April–June

Big appetite Bluefins gorge on smaller fish and reach an enormous size.

Big danger Because bluefins spawn in large schools, they are easily seen.

Big money Prized as sashimi, a single fish once sold for US$396,700 in Tokyo, Japan.

Humpback whale cows and calves stick close together on their long journey to the feeding grounds.

Bottlenoses and relatives

Acrobats of the sea

Jumping, flipping, twisting and spinning – dolphins have all these moves and more. Nearly 40 species of these aqua acrobats swim the oceans. The smallest is 1.2 metres long. The largest, the killer whale, or orca, is 9.5 metres long. Found mainly in shallower water near coasts, most dolphins stick close to home. Some migrate, but usually in response to changing water temperature or in search of food.

Bottlenose dolphin fact file

Type	Dolphin
Family	Delphinidae
Scientific name	*Tursiops truncatus*
Diet	Fish
Average lifespan	20 to 40 years
Size	Up to 4m
Weight	Up to 650kg

Bottlenose

Bottlenose dolphins range from Australia to North America, to Africa and Asia. They have an amazing ability to communicate and use pulsing sounds, whistles and tail slaps to keep track of each other and warn of danger. Some populations make seasonal migrations.

Teamwork Dolphins work together when feeding and herd schools of fish like cattle.

Jump for joy Dolphins leap to communicate, shake off sea lice and just for the fun of it.

Striped

Striped dolphins are easy to recognise because of their unusual markings. Black bands circle their eyes, and two black stripes run behind their ears. They can leap as high as 7 metres out of the water. They live in close-knit groups of up to 100 individuals or sometimes in schools of thousands. They migrate with warm-water currents in most parts of the world during the autumn and winter months.

Distinctive The striped dolphin's marks make it easy to identify.

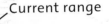

Current range

North Sea

EUROPE

Former range

Short-beaked

Relatively small compared to other species, short-beaked dolphins avoid cold water and typically live in more temperate areas. But lately large schools have been seen in the northern part of the North Sea. Scientists say this massive migration is the result of climate change. The short-beaked dolphins are moving farther north as ocean temperatures grow warmer.

Warming trend
The cold and misty North Sea is gradually getting warmer.

Chasing tuna Spinner dolphins (left) and spotted dolphins (right) have a unique relationship with yellowfin tuna. The species swim together in the Pacific Ocean. No one knows why, but fishermen rely on it. When they see dolphins, they set their nets. This causes a problem, however, because dolphins sometimes get caught along with the tuna. New nets and new laws are helping improve dolphin safety.

Salmon

Rivers of fish

Nine species of salmon swim the Pacific Ocean. Common names include kings, sockeyes, silvers and pinks. Salmon begin life as an egg laid in freshwater. They grow into smolts and migrate downriver to the sea. Then they swim back, returning to the place of their birth, which also becomes the place of their death. Some make a round-trip journey as long as 2,400 kilometres to complete the cycle of life.

King salmon fact file	
Type	Fish
Family	Salmonidae
Scientific name	*Oncorhynchus tshawytscha*
Diet	Insects, crustaceans, fish
Average lifespan	5 years
Size	840 to 910mm
Weight	4.5 to 23kg

Changing looks

Salmon undergo dramatic physical changes prior to spawning. Depending on the species, they may grow a hump or develop dog-like teeth and a curved jaw. Like autumn leaves, all change colour.

Migration

How returning adult salmon find the exact location of their birth after years at sea is still a mystery. Scientists believe their sense of smell plays a role. King salmon returning to central Idaho have a 1,400-kilometre journey that climbs from sea level to 2,100 metres in the mountains.

Spawning season

June–Sept

Growth Salmon grow rapidly in the summer and slower in the winter.

Spawning

Female salmon use their tails to dig shallow depressions called redds in the gravel. They then lay their eggs in them. A redd may contain up to 5,000 eggs. One or more males will fertilize them, and then the female covers the eggs with gravel. After spawning, adults quickly deteriorate in the freshwater, dying within a few days or weeks. The eggs remain protected in the covered redds. Rising water temperatures in the spring trigger hatching.

Yolk Blood vessels surround the yolk of the salmon egg; the black spots are eyes.

Eggs The eggs hatch into sac fry that grow around the remains of the yolk.

Few survive Only ten per cent of all salmon eggs will survive to become smolts.

Swimming upstream

SALMON RUN The annual return of salmon is a marvel of nature. The ability of the fish to find their way back upstream after a lifetime at sea is one of migration's greatest mysteries. Returning salmon have been an important part of human culture and commerce for centuries. Native Americans living in the Pacific Northwest have long celebrated and honoured them. A valuable commercial fishing industry was built on salmon migration. But even older is the connection between salmon and other animals. Many species depend on salmon as an important food source.

The bear facts Brown bears and grizzly bears rely on a diet of salmon to make it through the winter, as the fish provide them with a rich source of oil and fat. Before going into hibernation, bears eat as much salmon as they can. They stand in rivers as the fish migrate upstream and catch them with their paws and mouth. A big brown bear will eat eight to ten salmon a day; that is the equivalent of a young person eating 40 hamburgers at a time. Coastal bears that eat salmon grow bigger than those living in the interior. They have more cubs each year, too.

Farms and future The migration of wild salmon is being threatened. The populations of many of the nine species that swim the Pacific Ocean have declined dramatically as a result of overfishing, dams, logging and water pollution. Some salmon species are now raised in commercial farms in countries from Norway to Chile. While fish farms grow salmon for humans to eat, they do little to help provide food for animals like bears and bald eagles. Steps are now being taken to increase the wild salmon population for these animals.

Movable feast
Bald eagles, river otters and dolphins are just a few of the animals that depend on the arrival of wild salmon each year.

A rich diet of salmon helps grizzly bears store fat for hibernation.

European eels

Slippery change artists

European eels are fish, not snakes. They are not electric, either, but their journey's length and the changes they go through are shocking. Eels live in every European river that empties into salt water. They hide during the day and come out at night to eat. When it is really cold, they hibernate. After maturing, eels leave freshwater and swim up to 8,000 kilometres across the Atlantic Ocean to spawn.

European eel fact file	
Type	Fish
Family	Anguillidae
Scientific name	*Anguilla anguilla*
Diet	Molluscs, crustaceans, fish
Average lifespan	20 years
Size	Up to 100cm
Weight	Up to 9kg

Life cycle of the eel

Eels begin life as larvae in the open ocean. For the next one to three years, they ride the Gulf Stream. When they reach Europe's shoreline, they turn into tiny, transparent wigglers called glass eels. As they head upriver, their skin turns golden, earning them the nickname 'yellow eels'. After 10 years or more, they migrate back, changing color again. They reach the spawning grounds as silver eels, spawn, and die. The cycle starts anew.

Larva

Glass eel

Yellow eel

Silver eel

NORTH AMERICA

EUROPE

Atlantic

Sargasso Sea

AFRICA

Equator

SOUTH AMERICA

Ocean

Range of European eel

Ocean currents

Migration

No one has yet found exactly where European eels spawn. Most scientists believe it is somewhere in the Sargasso Sea, in the western Atlantic Ocean. One thing is for sure: the journey is long. Eels migrate in big groups. They swim 60 to 90 metres below the surface and can travel 50 kilometres a night.

Spawning season

March–June

Danger of extinction The population of eels has declined around 90 per cent since the 1970s.

Masters of disguise After coming ashore, such as on the coast of France (left), eels hide to avoid detection. They slide under tangled roots or beneath mud during the day.

Meal for others People are not the only ones who fish for eels. River otters, herons and cormorants eat them, too.

Walrus

Tusked travellers

Walrus may look funny with their bristly moustaches and blubbery bodies, but they are well equipped for life in the Arctic. Except for a short winter stay just beyond the pack ice, they are almost always on the move. Walrus are strong swimmers, capable of reaching speeds of more than 32 kilometres per hour. They have big appetites, too. A walrus eats 73 kilograms of clams and mussels a day.

Walrus fact file	
Type	Marine mammal
Family	Odobenidae
Scientific name	*Odobenus rosmarus*
Diet	Clams, shrimp, crabs, mussels
Average lifespan	20 to 30 years
Size	Up to 3.5m
Weight	Up to 1,800kg

Strength Walrus are strong swimmers. There are powerful muscles beneath the blubber.

Big teeth

Elephant-like tusks make the walrus a standout among its seal and sea lion cousins. Just like an elephant's, the ivory tusks are actually teeth that never stop growing. Both males and females have them, though the males' grow much bigger. They can reach more than 1 metre long and weigh up to 5.4 kilograms. Males use them for fighting, display and dominance. The strongest walrus with the biggest tusks usually rule the herd.

Migration

Pacific walrus spend the winter on rocky beaches and outcrops along the Bering Sea. The herds start moving north in April. Males and females migrate separately, and females give birth along the way. Calves weigh between 45 and 75 kilograms when born. The summer is spent feeding in Arctic waters.

Mating season   Calving season

Jan–March   15–16 months later

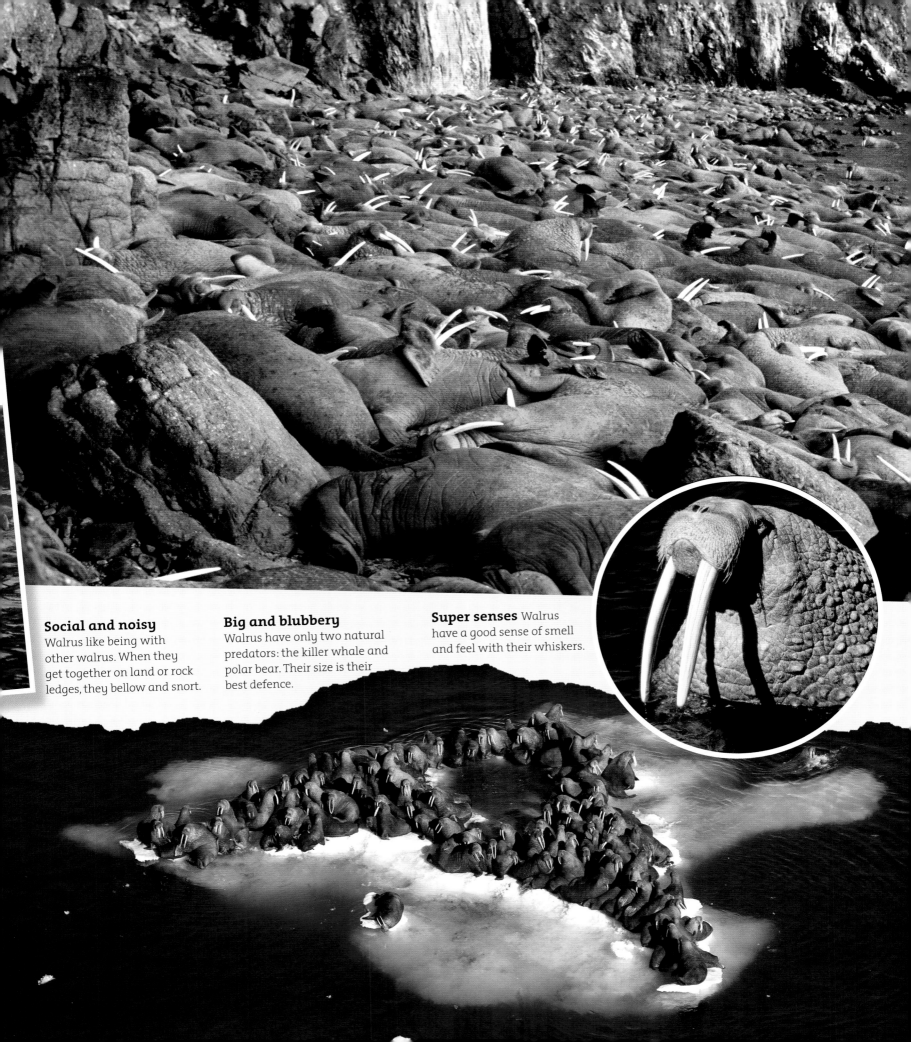

Social and noisy
Walrus like being with other walrus. When they get together on land or rock ledges, they bellow and snort.

Big and blubbery
Walrus have only two natural predators: the killer whale and polar bear. Their size is their best defence.

Super senses Walrus have a good sense of smell and feel with their whiskers.

Elephant seals

To the brink and back

Elephant seals are the largest of their kind. Two separate populations exist: the northern elephant seal migrates between Alaska and Baja California, and the southern elephant seal lives in waters just north of Antarctica. Hunting brought these giants close to extinction, but their numbers have recovered. Elephant seals spend most of their lives in the ocean feeding on the bottom. No other seal dives deeper.

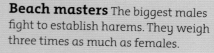

Northern elephant seal fact file	
Type	Seal
Family	Phocidae
Scientific name	*Mirounga angustirostris*
Diet	Fish, squid, octopus
Average lifespan	20 years
Size	Up to 6m
Weight	Up to 4,000kg

Proboscis

These big seals get their name from the male's enormous snout that resembles an elephant's trunk. Called a proboscis, it is used to produce loud roars when bulls fight each other over mates during the breeding season. The big nose also serves another purpose. The inside has cavities that reabsorb moisture every time the seal exhales. This allows the animals to stay out of the water for weeks at a time.

Beach masters The biggest males fight to establish harems. They weigh three times as much as females.

Migration

Elephant seals spend months at a time feeding at sea. Their travels take them up to 8,000 kilometres from the shore. They return to their rookeries on beaches in the winter to give birth and mate. Males arrive first to define and defend territories, and the winners collect a harem of 40 to 50 females. Breeding season lasts about three months.

Mating season — Jan–Feb

Calving season — December

Deep dive Elephant seals routinely dive 610 metres deep or more and can hold their breath for up to two hours.

Extreme cold
Southern elephant seals haul out on islands near Antarctica. Thick blubber keeps them warm in freezing temperatures.

Swim school
Weaned pups stay on the beach for a couple of months after their mothers leave. They spend this time perfecting their swimming skills.

Sea turtles

Riding the current

Among the oldest of all creatures, sea turtles evolved over 110 million years ago. Seven species still exist, but all are at risk of extinction. Fishing and building on beaches are part of the reason why. Sea turtles spend nearly all of their time in the water, coming ashore only briefly to lay their eggs. Catching ocean currents helps them when migrating. Some species, like the leatherback, travel across entire oceans.

Leatherback turtle fact file	
Type	Sea turtle
Family	Dermochelyidae
Scientific name	*Dermochelys coriacea*
Diet	Jellyfish
Average lifespan	45 years
Size	Up to 2m
Weight	Up to 700kg

Race winners Large flippers and a streamlined body make leatherbacks the fastest swimming sea turtle.

Leatherback

Leatherbacks are the largest of all sea turtles and are unlike most others. Their shell is not bony but, instead, is made of skin and oily flesh. Their flippers are the biggest in proportion to their overall size. The front pair can grow as long as 2.7 metres. Leatherbacks have the widest global distribution, too. They range from Norway to the tip of New Zealand. They are also the deepest divers, able to go 1,280 metres below the surface.

Cold waters An extra layer of fat helps leatherbacks keep from freezing in cold water like that of Alaska.

Migration

Leatherbacks travel from cold water, where they feed, to warm-climate beaches, where they hatch. Journeys average 6,000 kilometres. One sea turtle was tracked from its nesting site in Indonesia to California – a 20,000-kilometre trip.

Mating season	Hatching season
Various	60–70 days later

Global Leatherbacks roam the oceans widely, including to the waters off the Cape of Good Hope, South Africa (right).

Nesting and laying

Most sea turtle species return to lay their eggs on the same beach where they hatched years before. The female crawls to a dry part of the beach after mating and uses her front flippers to dig a shallow pit the size of her body. Then she shovels out an egg cavity using her cupped rear flippers and lays 80–120 eggs. She covers the eggs with sand when she has finished and heads back to the sea.

Sand tracks Gently sloping beaches make getting in and out of the water easier.

Darkness Turtles nest at night to help hide the eggs from predators like gulls.

Mad dash Hatchlings must cross the beach quickly to avoid predators.

Hatchlings

It takes a little over a month for the eggs to hatch. The temperature beneath the sand determines which sex the hatchlings will be. Temperatures warmer than 29.5°C produce females. Cooler temperatures produce males. Once the baby sea turtles break out of their shells, they waste no time heading for the safety of the water.

Atlantic EUROPE

NORTH
AMERICA

*Sargasso
Sea*

AFRICA

Ocean

SOUTH
AMERICA

Krill

The tiniest migrants

The largest migration in terms of sheer numbers is made by one of the smallest animals. Krill are shrimp-like creatures that float in the water. Their name is an old Norwegian word meaning 'whale food'. Krill are the biggest part of a baleen whale's diet. Other animals, including seals, penguins and squid, depend on them, too. In the Antarctic, krill are the engine that powers the ecosystem.

Antarctic krill fact file	
Type	Invertebrate
Family	Euphausiidae
Scientific name	*Euphausia superba*
Diet	Phytoplankton
Average lifespan	6 years
Size	6cm
Weight	Up to 2g

Ups and downs Most krill species undertake large daily vertical migrations in the water column.

Meals for many

Dozens of species of krill float in the oceans far and wide. The Antarctic krill is one of the most plentiful. Scientists say it is probably the most abundant animal species on the planet. Its biomass is estimated to weigh 500 million tonnes. During spawning season, swarms of Antarctic krill can cover up to 450 square kilometres of ocean to a depth of 200 metres. While krill occupy the bottom of the food chain, they support all the animal life above.

Water colours During Antarctic krill's spawning season, their density makes the water appear to be pink.

Big eaters Krill is the most important food for a baleen whale, which can eat up to 3.6 tonnes a day.

Special teeth Crabeater seals have developed teeth that let them strain krill from the water.

Bubble net Whales will work together to trap krill. They form a circle and blow a wall of bubbles.

Index

Photographs

Key: c = centre, r = right, l = left, b = bottom, t = top, cr = centre right, cl = centre left, br = bottom right, bl = bottom left, bc = bottom centre, tc = top centre, bcr = bottom centre right, bcl = bottom centre left, tcr = top centre right, tcl = top centre left, bg = background

ALA = Alamy; **ANT** = antphoto.com, **CBT** = Corbis; **FLPA** = FLPA-images, **FS** = Fabrice Simon, **GI** = Getty Images, **iS** = iStockphoto.com, **MP** = Minden Pictures, **NGS** = National Geographic Stock, **NHPA** = NHPA/Photoshot, **NPL** = Nature Picture Library, **SH** = Shutterstock, **SP** = SeaPics, **TPL** = Photolibrary.com, **UNEP** = United Nations Environment Program, **Wiki** = Wikipedia

79r **ALA**; 58b **ANT**; back cover tl, b, 1br, 16t, 17r, 20-21, 22br, 23t, 28cr, 30tr, 110-111bg **CBT**; 49b **FLPA**; 48cr **FS**; 2-3bg, 13tl, t, 24b, 24cl, c, 25b, 26-27, 28bl, 29b, 30cl, br, 31r, 32t, 34-35, 52-53, 78cl **GI**; back cover tr, 4cl, 8cr, bc, 9tr, tcr, 10bc, bcl, bc, br, 11tcr, bcr, br, 13c, cb, cr, 14-15, 15, 19tl, tc, 26l, 29c, 37bcr, 45tl, 54-55, 55bc, 56cl, 61tr, 63br, 64-65, 64c, cr, 66cl, 67tc, 67cr, bc, 71tr, 73tl, tr, cl, cr, bc, br, 79tl, c, bl, br, 80bl, 81tr, cl, cr, b, 84c, b, 85tr, c, 87bl, 94cr, bl, 95b, 96cr, cbr, 100tr, 103br, 107cr, 118bl, 119tc, 127b, 128br **iS**; 38-39, 50bg, 50cr **MP**; 2br, 8t, 9tcl, 12bg, 17bg, 20tl, 27r, 36-37b, 37br, 38tl, 39tr, 40l, 40-41, 42-43, 43cl, cr, 44-45, 46-47c, 47cr, cl, 48 c, cr, 49t, 51br, 58c, 75cr, br, 79tc, 82-83, 108b, 111c, 113t, 116c, 117t, 120bl, 121tr, c, br **NGS**; 4br, 8tc, cl, 9bc, bcr, 10cr, 11bcl, 12t, 13cl, 33bl, 39cr, 48b, 51tr, 56tcl, 59tc, 60-61bg, 62-63, 66c, bc, bcr, 67tr, 67c, br, 68-69bg, 68tl, 69tr, 70c, bl, cr, 71c, b, 72bl, 74-75bg, 80cr, 87tr, 91r, 92cr, 93tr, bl, 95t, 98bl, 99t, 100-101bg, 106cr, 107cl, 109tr, c, cr, 113bc, 114c, 116bl, cr, 118c **NHPA**; 8bl, 9tc, bl, 10t, 11tc, tr, 12br, 55br, 57cr, 60tl, 62cl, 63tl, tc, tr, cl, bc, 65br, 75tr, 75bcl, 79cr, 80c, 85tl, bl, 86tr, cl, bl, 94cl, 97t, bl, br, 99br, 101tr, 102bl, 103t, 104-105, 107tr, bl, br, 109tl, cl, c, b, 111cr, br, 116bc, 117bl, 119tr, c, cl, 121bl **NPL**; 1tl, 6-7, 13cr, 18, 19tr, 46cl, 46bl, bc, 47b, 65tr, 67cl, 72cl, 74bl, 75cl, 76-77, 80tr

The publisher thanks Puddingburn Publishing Services for the index.

Illustrations

Front cover by **Mick Posen/The Art Agency**

Cartography by **Will Pringle/Map Graphx**

Species silhouettes by **Peter Bull Art Studio**

25c **Argosy Publishing**; 87c **Markus Baader/MBA-Studios**; 94tr **Anne Bowman**; 47tc, 77br **Peter Bull Art Studio**; 36cl, c, cr, 92t, 93cl, cr, bcr **Leonello Calvetti**; 37t, cr **Robin Carter/The Art Agency**; 5tr, 56 (birds) **Dan Cole/The Art Agency**; 5cl, 57br **Barry Croucher/The Art Agency**; 59c **Christer Eriksson**; 27tl **Gary Hanna/The Art Agency**; 27bl, 41tc **Ian Jackson/The Art Agency**; 96c **David Kirshner**; 120t **Rob Mancini**; 41tr, br, 43bc **Polygone/Contact Jupiter;** 5r, 98tr, 99cr, 102c **Mick Posen/The Art Agency**; 85br **Kevin Stead**; 112c **Guy Troughton**

All maps and illustrations copyright Weldon Owen Pty Ltd.